SANCTUARY

Exploring the Magical
World of Birds

a memoir by
Kathleen Knight

Copyright ©2023 Kathleen Knight

All rights reserved.

No part of this publication may be reproduced, distributed, or transmitted in any form or by any means, including photocopying, recording, or other electronic or mechanical methods, without the prior written permission of the publisher, except in the case of brief quotations embodied in critical reviews and certain other noncommercial uses permitted by copyright law. For permission requests, write to the publisher at the address below.

ISBN #: 978-0-9966566-8-9

Published by Storyweaving Press

This book is the second volume of Storyweaving Press' special memoir series, dedicated to publishing books that document stories that matter, told to celebrate the complexity, delights, and discoveries of a life well-lived. If you have a memoir, or an idea for a personal memoir you'd like to create, contact the editor at cburbank@storyweaving.com.

PO Box 739
Accokeek, MD 20607

Cover and book design by Patrise Henkel
www.patrise.com

TABLE OF CONTENTS

Author & Founder Kathleen Knight 1

Beginnings 5

Chapter 1   The House in the Country 9

Chapter 2   The Raptor Center 21

Chapter 3   Tarrytown & the Great Pigeon War 33

Chapter 4   Roost 43

Chapter 5   Pidge 51

Chapter 6   Snowball 63

Chapter 7   Francis 73

Chapter 8   The Sanctuary 79

Profiles of Individual Birds 87

Chapter 9   Reginald 89

Chapter 10   Jewelene, Petel & the World of Pigeons 97

Chapter 11   Rob 105

Chapter 12   Billy 111

Chapter 13   Roost II: Passing 117

Chapter 14   Willow 127

Chapter 15   Nelly 133

Chapter 16   Gerald 139

Conclusion 145

Support Us 147

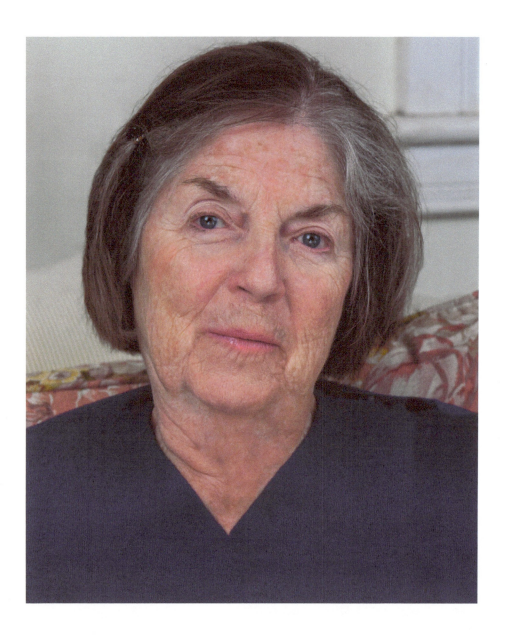

Kathleen Knight

AUTHOR & FOUNDER

The Sanctuary came into existence in 2007 as a result of my decision to honor a surprising close relationship with an injured wild pigeon I met. She had a badly broken leg when I found her on the ground; she was not releasable, and our relationship developed over several years. Through our friendship, and other experiences with these unique "people with feathers," I discovered how magical birds are as well as how poorly understood they are by most people. I decided to create a safe space for birds, and founded the Stonehouse Wood Sanctuary.

I wasn't always called to help birds. I grew up in St. Louis, graduated from Washington University, and came to New York to pursue a career in market research. It turned out that I eventually became CEO of the growing business my husband and I created. After some 25 years, my partners and I sold the company, which had grown to 25 times the size it had been when we started, with one hundred full-time staff. I stopped managing the company in 2000, and moved from the city to our country house, which ultimately became a sanctuary for more than 400 birds and countless wild creatures living on the land around the house.

During all this time, my passion for nature and the wonder it inspires has flourished. It is a real privilege to be so close to wild creatures of all sorts: birds, possums, skunks, and even bears. In that closeness, I see the fabulous gifts each creature brings, and how accurate the Native Americans have been in seeing each species and individual creature as a discreet source of wisdom.

Somehow that recognition is fading in our current world; it must not disappear. Those of us who recognize the value of the interconnected web of life must do what we can to support and protect that life process. The Sanctuary – and this book - is an offering to that purpose.

EXPLORING THE MAGICAL WORLD OF BIRDS

Beginnings

I could not have told you why I felt called to write this book. But soon I realized that I wanted to share stories of an ordinary life which has been astoundingly enriched by my connections with birds and the natural world. I also wanted to share my journey to build the Sanctuary, in hopes it would inspire readers to see birds in a new way.

So many people have not had an opportunity to meet bird individuals up close. It is difficult to understand them when you are always at a distance. Even in a flock, these creatures have their own paths and goals, just as humans do. Like us, each one has a unique personality and gift.

In writing this book, I discovered that each relationship with the birds brought me closer and closer to the wonder they represent. Each bird species has its own characteristics and preferences, of course; but that doesn't mean that individual birds are all the same. And although each bird's individualism may initially not be evident, over time it becomes very clear.

It has been an enormous privilege to know these creatures and that is why I am presenting this book, tracing my journey from the business world to the natural world and its stunning discoveries. And of course I am trusting that discovering birds like Snowball and Pidge and Roost will open the world a bit for readers.

I hope you will enjoy the journey.

EXPLORING THE MAGICAL WORLD OF BIRDS

The House in the Country

CHAPTER 1

The October day was misty; heavy grey clouds chased each other across the sky. The last leaves filtered down from the trees lining the narrow road. We had left the highway and were on muddy dirt roads that felt unsteady; the deep ruts and puddles let the car slide as if it had a will of its own. We wondered if we were lost when finally an old wood farmhouse appeared on a slight rise near the road, a tall maple tree at one corner. The tree seemed almost a part of the house; its three-foot trunk and spreading branches providing shelter, its remaining leaves a deep crimson. A second maple stood across the wet road near a pond bordering the forest beyond: a mixture of evergreen, maples and wild cherry trees.

The forest rattled gently in the rain and the fog lightened a bit. This was clearly the house the real estate agent had told us about. My husband Dick and I had been looking at houses for quite a while; we were a bit discouraged.

One of Dick's dreams had always been a country house. We decided this was the moment to find our place away from all the stress and struggle of the business world. The more we talked about it the better it sounded. We both recognized our precarious financial situation, but it did not matter. And so we set out.

Of course our hunt was harder and longer than we expected. If this was to be our dream of life away from life why was it so hard to find? It seemed like an endless struggle: houses too expensive, too small, too new, with not enough land, too near town or, a true limitation, no pond. I love water and I envisioned a pond for swimming. Then the agent called, bored with us no doubt, simply told us about the house and said we could go if we liked, but she couldn't meet us there.

But finally, at first sight, this house seemed to offer things we had decided we wanted: woods, no near neighbors and a dirt road. It was truly away in what felt like a place out of time. As we got out of the car the smell of wood smoke drifted out of a chimney, curling upward through the mist. The path from the driveway led up a few crooked stone steps to a side entrance. Lights glowed from the house offering the promise of warm dry comfort. When we went up the steps we saw there was also a path to a front door and we decided it was more polite to start there, so we climbed more steps, crossed a narrow front porch and knocked.

The owner came cheerfully to the door and invited us to come in. He was a stocky man, probably about fifty; we later found out he was the attorney for the village of Rhinebeck. They were selling the house so that they could be closer to the town. He and his wife were having tea in the kitchen and offered us some. Wonderful, we thought. We followed him through the pine paneled hall toward the back of the house.

We walked through a low-ceilinged dark room with small windows; it had a dining room table at one side, a small buffet cabinet and spindled Windsor chairs. The floor was dark wood; the whole room seemed to close in around us.

The house had started life in 1830 as part of a dairy farm; this room reminded us of other houses of this vintage we had seen and admired. There is something wonderful about a place that has survived so long and feels sturdy, comfortable and cozy still. We smiled to each other as we went deeper into the house. Looking ahead hopefully, we could see light, and stepped up through a small door into a cave-like kitchen where a fire burned in the wood stove.

The house had been built into the hill and a huge rock filled the back wall of the room gently curving down to the floor. The earth felt part of the house; the warm kitchen had small windows and felt like a stone haven. We had crossed into another time, safe from the weather and warmed by the burning logs from the forest. Dick and I just loved it; it set off an immediate deep sense of home. We had finally found our perfect idea of a country house.

The long search for the house started when we realized we wanted a refuge away from our intense business life. We were partners in a small but demanding market research firm and had been married a short two years. The years had been unexpectedly difficult as Dick's four teenage children were not pleased when he remarried after divorcing their mother. They were less than kind to me, thinking I had broken up their home. He said he had wanted a change for a long time, and had finally gotten a divorce. We married a year after the divorce and we were both briefly happy. But the level of anger and unkindness in my step-family was a great surprise to me and created considerable discomfort.

Additionally, the research business is always vulnerable to the economic winds and this was one of its shaky periods. We knew our endeavor was on uncertain ground and we were both working hard to build a reputation and a sturdy client base. We were marching along with determination, but we were tired.

But suddenly, there we were in the warm cozy kitchen in what seemed the perfect refuge from the chilly damp day and our frenzied lives. We were cautiously excited. The house had been there for 150 years, winter in winter out, and it felt settled, rooted. It was a two-story wood farmhouse with one large bedroom, two smaller bedrooms and a bath off the central hall upstairs. It had not only a pond but also a big barn and eleven acres, enough to provide privacy and a real exposure to field and forest. We smiled quietly at each other as we walked through the rest: the huge stone fireplace in the living room, the wide board floors upstairs, the ancient bathrooms, and a big cathedral ceilinged room at the back of the second floor which opened onto a road up into the forest. That room had bigger windows and another vast fireplace. The hill with its great rocky presence was right out the door, not ten feet away. The land and the house were well married. We sank gratefully into the old house with its quality of one time drifting easily into another.

We sold it to ourselves in about half an hour, scarcely believing our good fortune. It was accessible from our suburban house, surrounded by fields and forest, and utterly charming! We thought we could afford the mortgage. And it was so old and comfortable.

Somehow I did not realize what kind of decision adding another house was and certainly did not understand what "in the country" meant. I was more immersed than I knew in my business dramas, my new marriage and the trials of his angry extended family. I glossed over the fact that a new house in a new place would require creating some sort of life there in addition to the intense world we already inhabited. It turned into an Alice in Wonderland experience; everything was new learning. We had well water which requires electricity and a working pump, but electricity is not a certainty in rural areas. Oil delivery had to be planned. Telephone lines fail easily, and weekenders had to take their trash back home with them. In short, it was quite different from the orderly suburban world.

Among the surprises was the gun club just across the way. Unbeknownst to us it was hunting season; there was gunfire everywhere which would continue for another month until the season closed. A shock, all the guns, and the comfort and pleasure the locals experienced with them. We were startled, but not particularly alarmed.

When we bought the house we were already busy and feeling overwhelmed. Neither of us had not much spare psychic or physical energy for a big new project. Still, we lurched forward into our new adventure. Always when we got to the house and went into the kitchen we both felt captivated by its offer of something completely new and unknown; it felt inviting not intimidating.

In not too long it emerged that the experience of being intentionally in the country instead of passing through it had an impact I had not remotely imagined. Winter came quite quickly after we completed the buying process. Winter in the world of field and forest was a whole new thing. The land seemed to recede: first leaves and dead grasses, then cold then snow. The land felt less lively. Birds kept coming, either in migrating flocks or permanent residents who stayed and ate cheerfully at the feeders. I watched with worry as the snow grew deeper, wondering how such small creatures as birds could survive. But they did and they did not seem to become frantic; there was no vast flapping or panic.

I was frantic enough for everyone and worried every time the weather changed. I grew up in the treed suburbs of St. Louis and went to summer camp, but I never really had any relationship to the land so I did not have any idea I would be swept into the rhythms of the natural world by watching the weather and the birds. Along with the birds, deer came by the house, wild turkeys gathered across the road by the pond and raccoon and possum wandered past from time to time. I felt like Christopher Robin in his magical forest. In some basic way all was as it should be. I watched for hours as the light changed, the landscape calmed and the clear winter sunsets settled over the stillness.

What I knew of winter came from the city where snow is annoying: dirty, wet, and primarily in the way. In the country it turned out to be a blanket for the land offering protection from the ravaging cold. And for me, the cold wintry days in the country house afforded quiet times. I started to see how many colors and textures the fields held in winter: the grasses sticking up from the snow, red berries on the bushes and the skeletons of the trees outlined against the gray and white landscape. Suddenly I was deep in the beauty of the time, not frustrated by it. It was a turning point, though I did not realize that at the time. After the first year or so I saw that I was finding the world of the country more vibrantly interesting than the city.

SANCTUARY

Somehow when I was in the country I was in a different rhythm, and while it seemed slower because there were fewer tasks, it felt very complex and inviting. The birds endlessly ate at the feeders; the more I watched them the more I marveled at their survival skill. They seemed to know when storms were coming. In the day or two before a weather change the crowd at the feeders would be bigger and the feeders would need frequent refilling. In the storm, no one came to eat or forage. Then as soon as a break in the clouds appeared, feeder traffic began again. I never could see how these tiny creatures managed to withstand what I could not tolerate. It's all very well to say they know how, it is what birds do, but their achievement seemed a miraculous mystery to me.

Then I started to watch more deliberately, looking for the details, more fascinated by each moment. As time unfolded I noticed I had begun seeing them as inhabiting a universe different from mine but parallel. They had the survival issues I did, they had to find food and shelter, and mates and then worry about the babies and hope for the coming of spring. After I had watched enough to see how complex their situations where I developed a deep respect for their activity. In fact they went on from generation to generation as we were doing. I then saw that the trees had slowly given up their leaves and gone to sleep for the winter; the landscape was deeply still. And I, more and more interested in the stillness, began to settle into myself without effort.

I began to look forward to the Friday drive to the country. The last few minutes of the ride were on a narrow paved road from which we turned onto dirt roads through the forest which had been there in one form or another for hundreds of years. As we left the highway I felt whatever the business world had produced for the week fade away; I was truly away where the intense client service rhythms and their attendant conflicts slid soundlessly away. And the adventure of our fascinating new world began.

As time went on our lives evolved. We became better friends than married folk. The business became more of a business and much more orderly than it initially was. Slowly I found the weekly trek to the house difficult; our weekday lives were hectic, there was never enough time and going to the country to entertain each week became difficult. We still enjoyed the house and the company, but I found myself tired at the end of the weekend, not glad to have come out to the country. Eventually I refused to make the journey.

After thinking about it for a long time we decided to separate, found a mediator and dissolved the marriage. The change in our relationship had happened over time; we were not angry but no longer belonged together in the same way. The divorce simply formalized what had naturally evolved. We continued to be the best of friends for years and I have always been more than grateful that he wanted a country place.

I had become much more interested in the land, the forest and the wildlife and we agreed easily about the house. I was fascinated by the house; it seemed to have a life of its own that had gone on far before we arrived. The house felt so alive and yet I knew none of its stories, or how it had survived so well for so long.

SANCTUARY

While it was not particularly sensible when we bought it, the country house has opened doors to new worlds for me that I treasure. If not for the house, perhaps I would have taken a different road.

The Raptor Center

CHAPTER 2

One Saturday afternoon in our suburban house Dick and I were absentmindedly watching the television. A news spot came on showing a couple who had a raptor rehab center in a house they were renting nearby. Their landlord was about to evict them; they and the big birds were going to be homeless.

Both Dick and I were mesmerized watching the owls on perches behind the couple. I wrote down the information to reach them and we hatched the idea that we could rent the country house to them to help them out and to give ourselves a rest.

Off we went to talk it over. It was a bolt from the blue for them, and soon they were settling into the old house, amazed at their good fortune. We were delighted to be able to help the owls, hawks and ourselves at one swoop. They paid some rent which covered our small mortgage, and set about making enclosures for their birds outside and in the barn. The barn had five large horse stalls, running water and electricity; it was admirably suitable for bird housing and there was even a room for their clinic to treat the injured.

They had considerable knowledge about the birds and a gift for attracting volunteers. In all, they had about a 50% success rate with sending their rescued birds safely back into the wild. This was an above average achievement we were told, and we continued to be impressed by their determination and skill. Dick missed the house but approved of the bird folks; I too approved of them and was thrilled the house and land were put to such good use.

For five years or so it went well; we visited from time to time and were always greeted enthusiastically. The big birds were everywhere: in enclosures they had set up in the field by the barn, in the barn itself and the most fragile in the house. A large black turkey vulture named Elizabeth lived in a pen next to the barn, and periodically came out to greet visitors. She had broken a wing and could not fly, but was quite lively otherwise with shiny feathers and piercing eyes. Turkey vultures are scavengers, cleaners of the wild creatures killed one way or another. They are big with a broad wingspan and tend to gather in groups around a carcass and are often seen cruising the sky looking for opportunity. In some Native American traditions they symbolize transformation and rebirth, as their cleansing of the dead creates food for them and thus continues the cycle of life. Elizabeth was vigorous and in no way pitiful.

The owls were stunningly impressive. The injured in the house stood patiently with wings folded and eyes focused on whatever moved. They had taken over one of the bedrooms;

there were three there the last time I saw them. Their wild lives were interrupted by necessary confinement so they could heal. Even so, their wildness and inherent power radiated as they shook their feathers, rattled their wings and looked directly at me. And I looked upon them with sadness, hoping they were soon free again and if not, that they could adjust to a sort of assisted living facility.

Owls were new to me. I felt it a privilege to be close to such wild spirits, who even in these circumstances had presence and dignity. Silently I stood near these birds who had so recently hunted through the night in the forest, now enclosed, their power muted and their freedom curtailed, possibly permanently. What did they think, I wondered, as the lives they had known were out of reach?

The hawks had the same effect on me. They are daytime/twilight flyers and were more restless in their hospital settings in the house than the owls. They were clearly wild; sharp penetrating eyes watched, heads turned to confront what (or who) was coming. Feathers rustled, wings moved and their sharp claws shuffled on the perches. I found myself in the grip of magic looking at them. They came from a world I had only seen from a distance, and now they were less than three feet away, still beautiful and potentially deadly.

After a time with these injured raptors in the house, I had to go outside, saddened by the loss of their accustomed freedom. I went to see the shelters that housed birds who were in recovery. They were enclosed on three sides with the front open and wire covered. The birds had perches, logs and considerable room to move about, but no flying space. It was much easier for me to be with the outside birds, perhaps because they seemed almost at home in the shelters, although it did not feel as intimate.

Additionally, there were a number of hawks who had met with cars, electric wires and other obstacles. Hawks hunt in the daytime, and many of them were in outside cages, perched and watchful. All the big hunting birds have great vision and can see prey from distance and then move quickly. Often big red tails will cruise a territory, then wait in a tree for the target to move. They eat small animals and birds like pigeons and chickens. These birds had moved outside while they completely healed.

When I was near them I was aware of their savage beauty: fierce sparkling eyes, huge talons to grab food. The more I saw the more respect I developed for the role these predators played in keeping the balance in nature and how very skilled they were. Like the owls, the injured hawks were power interrupted.

In all there were about one hundred raptors at the raptor center. After some time the raptor center folks built a huge flight cage in the field by the barn so that the birds who were healing could build wing strength before being released. They would provide dead mice and other food so that the hunting skills could sharpen as well. Watching from the doors with excitement, I saw the birds swooping to and fro in the 40-foot-tall, 75-foot-long building. The increasing liveliness of the birds was tangible. A few flew only a few feet and then landed; others cruised the space with ease, recovering from the injury that had put them at the center.

And so it was that the Hudson Valley Raptor Center spent several years in our house in the country. Birds and volunteers were everywhere. The house, barn and land allowed the effort to grow and take in more birds. All was apparently going well, though the two center leaders were beginning to sound tired. Managing volunteers and fundraising was hard; I well understood their situation as it seemed parallel to our struggles with a growing business. Old systems that once worked suddenly fail because some circumstance has changed with new situations and challenges. That meant the leaders, who were at the core loving free spirits who wanted to help the beautiful birds, had to be executives. I admired their determination and their cause.

As I got to know their birds, I became aware I knew nothing about these remarkable creatures. My previous bird experience was much more superficial than I knew and now I was immersed in this deeply magnetic introduction. Though I did not realize it then, these birds were the messengers of mysterious new understanding. Because of them the whole of the natural world quite suddenly began to become more real and relevant day by day.

The time with the center offered a closeness with the big birds I had never known. In fact, I am sorry to say, I don't think I had quite realized they were actually alive and unique. As I soon discovered, my shallow attitude was not big enough to deal with what was going to happen next.

As Dick and I grew apart and separated peacefully, I suddenly felt a great affection for the country house and for the big birds who lived there. In the divorce agreement I bought the house from Dick but quickly got alarmed about my ability to keep it with only my income. Finally I decided to go see the raptor center owners and discuss the possibilities of their buying the property with my help.

We sat around the table in the dark kitchen on a rainy afternoon in the fall, wood stove warming what seemed a friendly conversation. I told them of our change of status and that I was uncertain that I could sustain the house and thought that perhaps they would like to acquire it as a permanent location. I said that while I had never raised any money I thought I probably could and would suggest we get a potential price from three different realtors and take the midpoint. It seemed fair to me and they thought so as well, they said. I said how much I admired their work and surely did not want to interrupt it, but needed to face potential reality. For all the help I would appreciate a seat on their board. They agreed to think about it and we all parted.

The next three weeks or so went by as I was traveling around the country with research clients attending focus groups, and I heard nothing about the house. Soon the phone rang in the office and it was the local newspaper, the reporter wanting to know if I had seen the article about the raptor center. No, I hadn't. Well, he said, you are an important part of the article but it is not a favorable portrait. It seems the raptor center had said that I wanted a lot of money for the property or I would evict them mercilessly as their previous landlord had done, and that I did not respect their efforts at all and certainly had no concern for the birds.

I was stunned and felt massively betrayed. I said to the reporter, "Well, I hope you have some time because I have a story to tell you!"

We talked for quite a while as he listened to my version of the situation, which he then printed as well. Of course, the couple from the raptor center were furious; no one in our community had ever suggested they were anything other than wonderful, caring for these impressive but wounded creatures.

The next few months were awful. Dick and I had several meetings with them to try to work the situation out, but there was too much sorrow and recrimination, accusation after accusation and no meeting of the minds. I offered to sell them a piece of land on which they could build a house of their own and lease them the land that held the bird housing and the flight cage. They thought that was yet another scam. My every contact may me sadder.

And now I was beginning to feel very selfish indeed. What would happen to the birds? Where would they go, and what would the center owners do? And I began to mourn the potential loss of the house very deeply, as I contemplated selling it, not for the raptors, but to anyone. I was surprised to care, but care I did, and deeply.

It was late winter and I was having dreams about the birds freezing and starving in the dreary cold. But then one day I realized that I had taken on all responsibility for everything and everyone, despite the reality that I had no true responsibility at all. But it was a pivotal moment. I had not given any thought to the notion that the birds themselves had individual lives with destinies. Suddenly I realized that they were entitled to these lives and I must give up thinking that I could plan everything for them. I had no understanding or thought of what they needed or wanted. And even if I did, I could not control their fates. I had to let go.

This event, difficult and upsetting as it was, taught me what I had not yet known; the wild creatures are individuals with needs and wants that only they understand. While I might think I knew all about them it was not true. I had never investigated their possible ideas or that they had any. I found it most embarrassing to have been so dreadfully arrogant as to not see at all what was directly in front of me; they were not objects at all and they deserve their own lives. I walked around the field looking at each of the birds with a very different perspective. They taught me an extraordinary lesson simply by their presence, as I woke up to their world. I was so delighted to begin to know them and now I have learned to watch carefully what I do with my bird companions, to give them the greatest freedom possible.

After this considerable shock, I concluded that my best choice was to evict the tenants, for my own sake and with the hope that the birds would find their way to the next refuge. I thought the raptor center folk would be better off with a place they owned, and in any event I wanted to keep the house, the land and the great lessons I had begun to learn there. In fact I was so excited by my recent learning that I could not wait to get started fixing the house and living there. After another unpleasant meeting I announced my attention to keep the property and to evict them. I tried to be civil, but it did not matter.

They took their anger out on the house, leaving it battered and in need of serious work. The wallpaper was coming off the walls and the renovations needed went beyond cleaning and painting. Further, they spread unpleasant gossip to all who would listen. They were furious, of course. No attorney wanted to evict them but I did finally find a lawyer who lived in a different town who would complete the process.

I was exhausted by the struggle of the eviction; but I realized that at last, the house was mine. There were no more thoughts of selling it, but much thinking about what it offered. It was a bit intimidating at first.

I immediately launched into the repairs, and the house began to clear of their anger and sadness. I added a giant greenhouse window with lots of light to bring in the landscape, expanding the living room to accommodate a new feeling of spaciousness and grace. The house now had a feeling of being married to the land rather than locked away with small windows.

And I could feel the release that had taken place. A serious and positive change had come to the old house and I was excited to begin my life there. It took four years to make it my permanent home, but my path to the Sanctuary had began.

RACING PIGEON

STREET PIGEON

Tarrytown & the Great Pigeon War

CHAPTER 3

I had been in my new house in Tarrytown for just over a year, and delighted with it. I was still getting used to owning both the Tarrytown and country houses. My Tarrytown home started life as a barn in 1882 or so, and was converted to a house in 1929. It looked small from the outside but was actually quite roomy, with high ceilings, large rooms, and a safe and sturdy feeling. The screened porch looked out over a large three-quarter acre yard with several huge trees. It was my first-ever home only for me — no husband, no family, just me and two refugee pigeons on the porch. In all honesty, I still felt odd and a bit uncertain in my new place.

I had taken the pigeons in that fall. Samantha, my good pigeon friend from the city, had recently and suddenly died. She had been with me for three years and was the first of her species I befriended. We met on the corner of 57th Street and Fifth Avenue in New York City after I had left a trying business meeting. In those days I was in the survey research business and was a senior partner in my company; complex and difficult meetings were not unusual but this one was exceptionally frustrating. I went to Fifth Avenue for a change of pace before dinner with a friend.

Outside Ferragamo there is a dry fountain and I sat on the edge of it, glumly resting. I was thinking about how untherapeutic shopping always was. I wasn't looking for adventure when I noticed a lump moving on the ground. As it got closer, it turned out to be a baby pigeon.

I said aloud: "If you need help I will do it. But if you don't, let's skip it. Give me a sign of some kind."

The lump scuttled across the pavement and stopped at my feet.

"OK!" I picked her up, grabbed my brief case and went to the garage to get the car. Providence had intervened, it seemed. I swiftly canceled my dinner date, and the pigeon and I went off to my house in Westchester about forty minutes north of the city. She settled on my lap on the drive; I had nowhere else to put her and she was quite calm.

We went to see my vet. He announced solemnly, "We should euthanize this bird. She has a bad leg and she was pushed out of the nest. She will not be releasable and any rehabber would agree with me."

"Well," I said. "Seems to me she managed to attract one of the few people who would even notice her, never mind want to help her. She got herself from Fifth Avenue to here and now she has arrived to you. Surely, the best next action is not to kill her."

He gave me a long look but he did not argue. In fact he hand fed her and cared for her diligently in his hospital for three weeks. She was soon well enough to come home to my new house, which we shared for about three years.

After her death, when the next two pigeons appeared, I did not hesitate. One was a homing pigeon who had been blown off course in a storm and come down in a friend's yard, then delivered to Tarrytown. I found the other wandering in a daze in Riverside Park in New York City. I knew he would not survive the night on the ground so I scooped him up and left him in the car while I went to dinner. Samantha had been helpless on the ground as well. Over my time with her I had come to be fascinated by the species.

I put both of them on the porch, big enough so they would have room to fly and in general recover. As it got colder I put up plastic tarps to shelter them from the wind, which is dangerous for birds. The porch was in the back yard and not visible to anyone but me because of the dense shrubbery. It seemed to fit the bill for the present.

The porch arrangement would work only short term, though. Soon I decided to build a small coop for the birds in my big yard and applied to the zoning board for approval as required. It never occurred to me anyone would object. The zoning board sent out notices to the neighborhood, allowing for comment. And the objections were many and various.

The house was set in a courtyard of four houses, and had a communal gravel drive of perhaps two hundred feet coming in from the paved street outside an ancient low stone wall. My house was farthest from the street and looked like an ordinary cottage from the outside. But once inside, the old house and its big trees seemed to offer a place with its own magic. When I bought the house I was so entranced I didn't even notice the proximity of the other houses; later I realized how close the other neighbors were and what that might mean. It never occurred to me that such deep conflicts might surface.

Three of the courtyard neighbors began creeping around in my yard looking at the porch and scowling at the birds. They did not ring the bell or visit to talk over my plan; they simply snooped. It felt like a suburban version of the Salem Witch trials, with enraged villagers and frightening potential outcomes. The first creeper was Gordon, a retired postal clerk who had always hated and feared pigeons, and the second his good friend Sieggy the wife of a German diplomat across the way. Emily was half of the couple in the cottage facing the street; they seemed nice but had an unfortunate tendency to feed feral cats, unwelcome guests who haunted the bird feeders looking for dinner. The terror wasn't universal. Emily's husband, Greg, was an environmental reporter on a Westchester paper and a believer in freedom of choice, so he didn't interfere.

As the town's notices spread through the neighborhoods, I rapidly discovered I did not represent the majority view. I was astonished and wounded. Gordon's anger, in particular, was a little frightening. My neighbors seemed to think some great evil was about to take place, and I was the enemy of the courtyard. I realized I had somehow set off an incident of unexpected proportions.

I was still running a research business at this point, and I had a long conversation with my partner about what to do. He was not a pigeon lover but he did not approve of the neighbors' creeping and the town's negative attitude. He had spent time in Democratic party politics in the city and was quite astute. I had also worked for political campaigns before I moved to New York, so between us we had some experience. I set about thinking about the situation as if I were running for election.

I called every medical authority I could think of to find out if pigeons really did carry disease or if these were just rumors. I talked to the NY Office of Public Health, the Mt Sinai Hospital Infectious Disease Unit, the Animal Medical Center in New York City and the Centers for Disease Control in Atlanta. All of these experts gave me their names, titles and permission to quote them. They confirmed pigeons just had a bad reputation with no truth behind rumors of disease and destruction.

My next effort was to recruit local pigeon flyers to come and testify to the stability and vibrancy of pigeons. But this group wanted no part of anything public. I moved on the national pigeon associations: same response. I came to realize these people understood what pigeons represent to the general world far better than I did.

In a further unfortunate development, it turned out there was man on a nearby street who had an actual flock of homing pigeons which he treasured. He was a janitor by trade and terrified that someone would see his birds and take them. And now it had happened; the town was in an uproar over my pigeons, and he might lose his. That did it. I resolved that no matter what, I was not going to be the cause of this man losing his beloved birds, who were hurting no one and lived in spotless surroundings in his back yard.

Suddenly, the pigeon issue – and I along with it — had gotten famous. I was interviewed by the county paper, then by a radio station. I received a number of unsolicited letters of support before the zoning board meeting. They moved it the largest room in the town hall because they expected a large crowd. I called my neighbors outside the courtyard as a friendly lobbying effort, but discovered pigeon phobia everywhere. One woman, a force in the local Republican party, was offended that a wild town pigeon flock occasionally rested on her roof, cooing and otherwise demoralizing her, apparently. She vowed to muster support for a ban on pigeons.

Meanwhile on the back porch, the two birds continued cheerfully, unaware of the pending dangers. I was in a state. I just wanted to live in my stalwart house with my two pigeon rescues. But there was nothing for it but to present an nonthreatening face to the town on behalf of my birds, and to help my new friend protect his flock. I put together a presentation for the zoning board as if they were paying clients: charts, bullet points of evidence, commentary about the unjust suspicions of imminent disease and so on. I dressed for a client presentation to prevent being stereotyped as a 'fringe' type, gathered my small group of supporters, and nervous but determined, went to the meeting.

It was a full house. I presented for about twenty minutes and the janitor spoke impressively about his healthy pigeon flock. Our supporters talked about what good people we were, and Greg, my one supportive neighbor, talked about how foolish it seemed to fight over two birds, that it was no one's business but mine, that I took good care of my property, and all of this was invasive and silly. My lawyer testified that there was no menace whatsoever to the community. The birds' opponents announced that they didn't want any more pigeons, and if the town approved my coop, it would be the first of many such disasters to beset the otherwise pure Tarrytown. After the event, my neighbor Republican walked out with my lawyer, announcing, "I can coo louder than you can!"

The lawyer, no doubt hoping I was willing to let it go, asked how serious I was about this. I said, "I am not going to have my friend lose his birds because of this. Whatever it takes, I'll help."

The town meeting was televised for the citizens and got a lot of attention in the local papers as well. I got more letters and a few unexpected calls, and made another appearance in the newspaper. The bad news was that all the coverage meant the town scheduled a second hearing. More citizens apparently had more opinions.

After the second meeting, a replay of the first, there was a long, quiet time while the board deliberated. During that time I realized that I was elementally upset, no longer felt safe in my house, and feared for the birds. I finally saw that either I had to forgive the neighbors and really mean it or I was going to have to move. Initially, I decided on forgiveness. About the same time, the town concluded that the house for the pigeons was not acceptable and henceforth domesticated pigeons would not be welcome in Tarrytown. However, there were two permanent exceptions: the gentleman with the flock and my two birds.

My interest in pigeons and my respect for them continued, together now with a sadness that misunderstood creatures could be so hated. I gradually forgave my ignorant townsfolk, and began to establish casual relationships with the creepers. The pigeons settled into their new coop.

One night in early summer I heard a loud noise at about four a.m. and went to check on the birds. There was a big hole in the screen and one of the birds was gone. The homing pigeon had been taken by an owl; I found his remains the next day. I suspected he would not have been happy in captivity in the long run because homing pigeons want to home. His owner had died and the secretary of his racing club (named on the band on his leg) had suffered a heart attack and would not accept the bird back.

I quickly found a pigeon fancier to take the other bird before an owl could catch her, too. He was a gentle man, with about fifty pigeons. He stayed carefully under the radar to ensure the neighbors didn't harass him and his birds. He was glad to take the bird who shortly after arrival found a mate, laid eggs and produced chicks. A fine next step, I thought, after a challenging learning experience.

A long time later I realized how important those troubles had been. For one thing, they taught me how far most of us are from nature and how dangerous it therefore feels to welcome wild creatures into our communities. My neighbors imagined two little pigeons were a threat! It was clear I needed to find a more welcoming place.

And now, years later, the Stonehouse Wood Sanctuary houses about three hundred and fifty pigeons in Rhinebeck, New York. There, they do not find pigeons dangerous. I have often thought that had I not faced Tarrytown's prejudices, I would quite probably not have created the Sanctuary, a fascinating and satisfying home for me and the birds. All this shows you can't know what will happen around the next bend. It is best never ever to give up.

Roost

CHAPTER 4

As time went on, I spent more time at the farmhouse and I began to feel part of the place. From the greenhouse sun room I could be a close observer and felt like a crony of the wild creatures who went by. The bird feeders attracted pileated woodpeckers, cardinals, doves and all sorts of other birds. Deer, wild turkey and possums came by. In all, it was enchanting to be so much a part of the natural world.

There was a big screen porch as well, where the long sunset of the summer evening allowed for a peaceful time as the bird and squirrel sounds of the day settled cheerfully into the evening chorus of frog and coyote from the swampy part of the field across the road.

By that time I had become deeply interested in birds and had created an aviary off the front porch. It was about fifteen feet by ten feet and was attached to a small but sturdy shed I purchased from the Amish vendor nearby. The lovely white doves I had rescued from small cages in pet stores had settled there. They cooed peacefully as evening came.

One day I was coming back to the house from an errand at the hardware store when I noticed a rooster and three hens in the grasses on the side of the road. The rooster had magnificent green black feathers with a collar of long buff feathers cascading over his sides. He was clearly the leader of the small group as he stood proudly with them, head up, tail erect and feathers shimmering in the afternoon light, his hens scratching in the dirt beside him. I was delighted at the chance to watch the little group and to discover that they did not immediately run off. I wondered where they had come from since no one on the road had chickens, nor had I seen any on the neighboring roads.

Next day, there the little group was again. They were scattered, but complete. In truth, I had thought about them quite a bit since I had first seen them and hoped they would find refuge. Chickens have always interested me. I was charmed whenever I saw a flock of them in a yard. And so it went for several days; I would go to look and see how they were doing.

One by one, the hens disappeared. After all, I said to myself, it is the country; the fox and coyote have to eat too. I wasn't happy though. Finally there was just the rooster. I was worried he too would be dinner for a predator or go hungry.

In the next few days he came quite a way toward my house from the corner where I first saw him; I began to hope I might entice him to my place with food and water. He would be safe there, I decided. However, the rooster appeared on the verge of the old dirt road only during the daytime. By evening he was gone. He seemed to be spending nights in the large field across the road, which is also home to lots of local creatures, including a group of active and noisy coyotes. I saw the rooster go off into the field at night and reappear every morning.

Each day I dropped sunflower seeds in the road, with the largest batch, closer and closer to the house. After about three days, there he was in the yard. I was excited: a visiting rooster in my side yard! He was a true symbol of country life. In old stories the farmhouses always have chickens in residence. Now I put out lots of seeds and fresh water. Success!

Soon he began his morning rooster call loudly over the yard. He seemed so magical – free, independent and proud, always striding around as if all the world was his. I began to wait for him and to worry about him each night: where was he going? Would he be safe?

But he did come every morning about seven and crowed outside. I happily went to meet him with sunflower seeds as he waited outside the back door. Day by day we began to get to know each other; he seemed more and more to belong, digging for bugs in the garden, investigating all around the house, eating under the feeders for the wild birds and in general making the land his. But each night he went back to the big field on the other side of the road and each night I said prayers for his safety. The coyotes howled vigorously in the swampy end of the field. I feared for Roost, as I had begun calling him.

I admired his survival skills; everyone else in his group was gone and he was still here. I was honored to be a destination for such a regal individual. All was well, except for the approaching fall when the warm August would inevitably chill into winter. Winter in my area is true winter. I could not see how he would survive. Still, every evening he strode off purposefully into the field.

After two weeks of this I hatched a plan: I would lay a trail of seeds into the aviary off the front porch and if he followed, he would be safe there in a new home. I took up watching him from the comfort of the wicker porch chairs and started talking to him in the afternoons. The ten or so white doves in the aviary seemed interested in him too, as they sat and watched whenever he was around, chattering to each other. In all, it made for a comfy bucolic scene and felt quite the right thing for the old farmhouse.

After a week or so I decided it was time. It was a lovely summer day with clear blue sky, drifting light clouds. I nervously laid out the seeds, settling a big seed stash and water inside the aviary and waited for afternoon. For the past few days, as the sun started to settle gently over the big field, he had come around the house scratching. Then he would cross the road for the night, settling on some low limb he had chosen in the field. I told the doves what I was planning; I hoped and trusted they would not dash out the door I had to leave open for Roost, or call too loudly.

Suddenly, there he was at the corner of the porch. I took a deep breath and got on the lush green grass between him and the road. We looked at each other for a moment or two and then I started ambling slowly from side to side interrupting his usual route to the field, helping him discover the seed trail to the aviary.

It was a tense half hour. Several times he looked up wistfully at his usual path toward the field, but he made no dash for it. He kept inching toward the doves on the perches high in the aviary. Mercifully the doves were quiet, seemingly content to be spectators.

And then, wonder of wonders, he was inside. I closed the door, called out a gleeful "Welcome to your new home, Roost!" and collapsed onto the grass for a good cry.

Next morning and for each morning thereafter, he crowed, letting all the rest of us know the day had begun. And that he was simply present. It seemed so wonderfully cozy – not just any old rooster but one who had chosen this place as a refuge, at home with the 10 or so white doves.

Doves feed on the ground but mostly live on high perches. Roost was mostly a ground dweller, though he liked to get up on the old tree limbs that I had put in the center of the aviary. All was well. But after a week, I realized he was alone even though he was surrounded by birds. Birds accept companionship of other birds, but they like to be with others who are like them. They then create their own community and seem joyous within it. Magnificent Roost had no community. He had friends in the doves, me and the wild birds, but no hens. My idea of comfort had provided safety, but possibly not contentment.

By now it was a radiant October and the county fairs and their poultry shows were in full swing. I took a picture of Roost and went forth to discover what breed of rooster he was. The chicken world has a very large number of different types, and it seemed better to find hens for him of his type if possible. The gods smiled, and there, in the Columbia county fair poultry exhibition, was a rooster who looked exactly like Roost, and who was being shown by a local fancier. Four Phoenix hens soon came to live with us. The hens clucked wildly when they saw Roost and he strutted proudly, tail and head held high. I felt like a proud aunt, watching her relatives enjoy themselves.

Roost and his flock of four settled in happily with the doves; all was well. This new experience, and my profound connection with Roost and then his ladies was exciting. I had never known an animal who was so active and engaged, digging worms, chattering to his flock, and protecting them from danger. He was comfortably in charge and the hens depended on him.

When the hawk flew over, Roost pushed them all into the bushes so they were invisible. When it was safe, he led them out. I felt most honored to be close to his ways, and watch a new way of living unfold in our shared days. It was clear he felt at home, keeping his flock in the yard and in the aviary.

I knew Roost well for several years; his life evolved, as did mine. It was a great privilege to witness this bird's proud determination to be the leader, and experience his evident trust in me. I have loved chickens ever since my lessons from Roost began.

The rest of Roost's story will be in Section Two.

Pidge

CHAPTER 5

It was a damp chilly day. The gray jumbled sky carried little reminder of summer. The road curved through the old reservoirs, winding toward the town. I had a lovely swim and was driving slowly home. As I rounded the bend, I sensed a bird on the ground, rustling anxiously, just inside the railing that divided the street from the woods around the lakes. I considered leaving well enough alone, but stopped — something was wrong. The rustling seemed like struggle, and I wanted to see if help was needed. There began the great Pidge adventure.

Most people with whom I have discussed pigeons hold them in low esteem. I have history with pigeons, or perhaps I would not even have noticed the small creature. The great gentleness I have found seems to have escaped most people's notice. Of course, like most humans, I did not recognize their true worth at all until I got to know one very well. I picked Samantha up when she fell out of her nest near the corner of 57th Street and Fifth Avenue in New York City. I knew nothing much about birds and had never met a pigeon before. However, as she and I were together for several years I came to treasure her and missed her greatly when she died suddenly, apparently of a respiratory infection, according to the emergency vet. It was to be three more years before I met Pidge.

As I got closer to the rustling on the ground near the lakes, and not far from my upstate suburban home, I saw the familiar pearl gray of an ordinary pigeon. When I bent to pick him up, he did his best to escape, flapping and dragging himself across the ground, a wild thing determined to get away, but not really able to get far. After following him for a bit I scooped him up and took him home, wrapped in a towel I keep in the trunk of the car. He was not pleased, but was too weak to argue much. One of his legs was broken and he was very thin under his feathers. I feared he might be close to death.

We got home. I taped up the leg, got an old cage from the basement, and did my best to make a comfortable resting spot on the back porch with old towels for a bed. At least it was not so damp and cold as being on the ground. I dissolved a bit of antibiotic in water (easily obtainable for birds – no prescription needed) and gave it to him. I gathered bird seed from the supply for the other birds in the house and sat back to watch.

He was a bit tentative at first, but he was so hungry that he overcame caution. He ate quite a bit, had a good deep drink of water and seemed better. His eyes no longer had a frightened startled look. I sat with him for a long time, just watching the wild creature begin to revive; he seemed more alert and was settling into the towels. I didn't think he was giving up; he was calm, looking around and breathing easily. It was getting dark. I covered the cage for the night, wished the bird well and hummed a bit as I went in.

Next day, first thing, we took a trip to a vet with whom I have long experience. He is a person of high competence and great heart, but he is practical. He said, "This bird should be euthanized. Any rehabber would know that."

"Well," I said, "I don't know that. He managed to get my attention and now he has gotten to you. Seems like an accomplishment to me. So, we are not going to ignore all that and kill him. We are going to do what we can to help him live, and if he chooses not to, then fine. But he will have had a chance. "

I left the bird at the vet's and went off harrumphing. "Kill him indeed!" I muttered to myself.

We would wait to see if the bird was staying in this life or going on to the next. I found myself very excited by the possibility of his survival. It would be fun to have a pigeon again. My experience with Samantha had been fascinating. Because she was so young when I found her, she decided I was her family and so she was very affectionate, following me everywhere and loving to sit and view the world from my shoulder. I was charmed by the trust she offered. We became close friends. I was now interested to see what the experience of an adult bird would be, one who had a life as a free wild creature, now in a different circumstance.

The wounded bird had captured my full attention even in our short acquaintance. When I found him on the ground he showed such courage. Even though he couldn't walk and no longer had the strength to fly, he was struggling to escape me, a suspected predator. Would I have been so valiant in the same circumstance? I'm not sure. It seemed a significant privilege to be participating in his life.

Days went by. The bird was at the vet, getting antibiotics, having the bottom part of his broken leg amputated and starting to recover. I got phone calls from the office reporting progress. It appeared he was not going to die just yet. Finally, after two weeks it was time for him to come home.

By now, it was too cold for the cage on the screen porch. The best possibility was the dining room table. A number of birds lived at my house at this time – cockatiels with newly hatched babies and two different kinds of doves. My relationships with these creatures had all started in the same way – some creature appeared to need help, a bigger cage, a safe refuge or some calling out that I seemed increasingly to hear. My first cockatiel came because the next-door neighbor was moving to Florida and thought his bird would not survive the flight. I took him. The flock expanded over the next few years but except for the pigeons there were no wild birds.

I wondered what would become of the pigeon; would he be lonely? Would he die after all with no flock and not much freedom? But home he came and began to eat fiercely in his new territory, my former dining room table. Six diamond doves would be his near neighbors, lovely small gray brown creatures of great delicacy and considerable cooing who lived in a five-foot flight cage against the dining room wall, occasionally fluttering back and forth, and calling to each other all day. Before the dove's arrival, the room had been a formal dining room with a chandelier, flowers and vines painted in the panels on the walls and silver in the buffet. As my time for formal entertaining seemed to have passed, I enjoyed the doves along the wall, and then let the pigeon claim the dining room table without a second thought. I waited to see what would develop, but I was hopeful.

Animals have been my teachers for some time, and each one offers a gift. Some time back I stopped seeing other creatures as "pets." To me they feel like interesting beings who happen not to speak English or go to the office, beings with real lives, personalities and destinies. I feel blessed by my relationships with them. For example, cockatiels, small parrots with a head plume and a brilliant orange spot on their cheeks, are determined and pushy. They make noise when anyone comes in the house, chatter to each other and flutter their eight-inch wingspan to make their presence known. Relative to the other birds, they are smart and regularly solve the problem of how to get out of the cages if I am not paying attention. They have quite a good sense of personal boundary, and if another creature invades, they push back at once. The more I watch this behavior the more I admire the clarity they have with each other.

The other birds I had experienced were doves —large white doves and the familiar pale brown ring neck doves. The different doves all share a quiet peacefulness. They are quite still a good bit of the time – they walk quietly, usually slowly, and speak softly to each other from time to time. There is none of the excited chatter of the cockatiels. Even the little diamond doves who often coo cheerfully are not raucous – they produce a melody that ripples through the house with great beauty. In all, doves seem by nature quite happy in their surroundings – they are not trying to escape their cages or from each other. In the Buddhist sense, they just are. If they sense a danger, they respond as a group with warning cries until the danger passes. Then they again return to their ordinary state of peacefulness. An achievement, I think. I have been meditating for years and seldom have long periods of the still state of being which comes so naturally to the doves.

The pigeon joined the household, adjacent to the dove community. Since he would not be returning to his wildlife, I named him Pidge. He seemed to gain strength and to be managing well on one leg. He would tolerate it when I picked him up, but he was clearly not a pet. He was standoffish and wanted to avoid being handled too much. I was nonetheless enthralled and continued to feel pleased to have a wild creature becoming part of the household. Adventure!

Over the months, Pidge grew healthier and became interested in the whole household; he would visit the other birds, and they appeared to be exchanging views. I liked the feeling of community that was developing. By the next June, when the birds and I were going to the country for the summer, Pidge turned some kind of inner corner. Suddenly two eggs appeared in her nest and I realized that he was actually she. Although her eggs did not hatch, she had settled in. (Female birds do not need to have mates to lay eggs; these eggs were not fertilized.)

At about the same time, she became very affectionate with me. One day when her cage door was open she flew out of the dining room to join me on the couch in the living room. I was surprised and delighted. I felt trusted and accepted by this unusual and exciting creature. After that, she liked nothing better than to sit in my lap and participate in whatever I was doing. She came to find me wherever I was in the house. Gone was her standoffishness, the wildness, the distance. Perhaps she had decided I was her flock after all. She began to cheerfully and persistently investigate any other humans who appeared. This was surprising for some of the folks, since birds are not easy for everyone. People who like predictability seemed to become nervous with an uncaged and thus unmanageable bird flying about. Pidge didn't mind; she liked to meet new people.

In fact, Pidge became particularly fond of my business partner, a warmhearted man who grew up in New York City. He had a city person's dark view of pigeons. He tried quite hard to be polite, but it was tough. Whenever he came by, Pidge wanted to be with him, immediately landing on his shoulder for a visit. He was glumly tolerant but not happy. However, even he found her a captivating presence, commenting "Well, it certainly isn't dull here," with a grim chuckle.

Meantime, Pidge and I became closer and closer. She was gentle, generous and above all, peaceful. Sitting on my shoulder; she felt like a warm feathered heating pad. Hours went by as we sat on the porch in the long summer twilight and took in the lush landscape of the country. Occasionally the wild bird she had been reappeared – when the hawk was nearby or the coyote howled. Then she instantly became alert, watchful and waiting for the next event. The peacefulness was gone, replaced by vibrant readiness. I was completely fascinated by seeing her so clearly live in the moment.

Her ability to be fully in the here and now was her great gift to me. She adjusted completely to her new life, so radically different from the woods where she started. She lived indoors and took up with humans. Birds are not like mammals and certainly not like dogs; they choose to have a relationship with you or there is no relationship at all. This creature clearly chose to let her old life go and move fully to her current one. I admire that ability very much. I find much smaller changes alarming in my own life.

Over my time with Pidge I too learned to be still for long times and to drop fully into the experience of the present: the eternal rustle of trees, the chat of wild birds, the bark of the coyote, and to realize that each of these was a world within itself. I had been moving too fast and bustling too much to be connected in the way I learned from Pidge. It was her nature to be an integral part of anywhere she was. I cannot think of a better way to be.

Pidge and I were together for perhaps seven years. During that time I got to know pigeons well and to realize that while she and I had a close relationship, I was just not a pigeon and she missed her own kind. I decided to help by introducing another pigeon but it did not go well. He was not interested in a handicapped, older bird and rejected her forcefully; he pecked at her, pushed her under a chair and then just walked away and flew up onto a chair, ruffling his feathers and sending forth a deep growl. I felt sad for her and for me - I had such hopes for the relationship.

I had not yet learned that a wounded or injured bird is always seen as a danger to the whole flock and so is ostracized. That is likely what happened to her after her leg was broken. The other birds and I were a substitute flock for a good long time, and then, suddenly, not. She began to seem frail and then to have respiratory issues (common in birds) and in general to decline. She could no longer fly upstairs, though she would try. She grew weaker and finally quite peacefully died.

I was heartbroken and not only missed her but felt sad that she had not had a flock of her own or pigeon companions. After thinking it over for quite a bit I decided to honor her memory and the great gift of her trusting and deep friendship by taking in a few refugee pigeons in my country place. I could easily put up some housing. It seemed a fitting acknowledgment and celebration of a life changing experience.

Several years and many experiences later, I established the Sanctuary on my farm in the country. My idea of helping out a few pigeons grew gradually, and now there are over four hundred birds here. Most are pigeons, but there are also doves, chickens, a few turkeys, geese and pheasants. They are all housed in coops around the old 1830 farmhouse, and they are doing a very important thing; they are living lives that are supported (in the sense of food and shelter) but not managed. For the most part, they are in charge of themselves. The pigeons come out to fly and those who want to leave can, and those who want to stay can. Their lives belong to them.

I have been repaid for my effort many times over by the sense of peace and liveliness that surrounds the old farmhouse where I now live full time. It is all a great and continuing surprise. I first met Pidge after my divorce, but before I sold the market research business, which by now served primarily Fortune 500 clients.

I remember that when I finally sold the business, my business partner said "Gee, you aren't going to be a crazy pigeon person, are you?"

"Maybe" I said. "Depends how you look at it."

Snowball

CHAPTER 6

A lot of bird people know about Stonehouse Wood Sanctuary, and I often get alerts about creatures in need of permanent or temporary homes. If I have room, there's no question. Sometimes I make room, and I rarely, if ever, regret the stretch.

One day the pigeon rescue guy in New York City called about Snowball and her flock of six pigeons, and their companion parrot. Their person had end stage lung disease, lived on a 5th floor walk-up in the Village and had to go into rehab. Foster care was needed for a two-month period, after which they would all go home.

From the beginning, that plan seemed overly optimistic. An end stage diagnosis meant that their person, Bobby, was unlikely to return to good enough health to manage his whole collection. We talked together, and I suggested that he consider letting me place the five pigeons in my large flocks at the Sanctuary and find a home for the parrot. (Parrots can have very long lives - 65 years is common- and so a stable home would be a relief to the bird and to Bobby.) Together, we decided that

Snowball would be the only temporary resident, as he was Bobby's favorite bird.

Snowball had come to Bobby in a snowstorm some three years before and he had taken her in off the fire escape. They had become close friends over their time together. He seemed downright relieved that the other birds could join my Sanctuary flock, and that we'd found a good home for his parrot. He wanted to know everything about Snowball's stay; where would she live, and could she be kept separate and indoors?

At this point in my pigeon experiences, I had taken in at least 100 birds from one place or another and so I was not concerned, except by the somewhat unsettling nature of the nephews, who soon arrived with the entire flock. They were large, burly, silent men around forty, dripping wet from the cold spring rain. The birds had been wrangled into boxes, but seemed none the worse for the journey. I know from experience that capturing and boxing that number of birds is not easy as the birds are not usually cheerful willing travelers.

The two men grumbled about the weather and the birds as they trudged into my Tarrytown house, apologizing for the mud they tracked in, and thanking me for "taking de birds from Uncle Bobby." They peered furtively around them, looking down as if hiding a secret. Somehow I felt I was participating in a somewhat suspect television show in which the birds would turn out to be dangerous and nothing more would ever be heard from their delivery men. It was probably my imagination, but it all felt odd and I was a bit nervous even after they left.

The adventure proceeded as planned, at least at first. The birds and I went to the Sanctuary in Rhinebeck, where every new citizen went into quarantine for thirty days. This is normal practice as a health safety precaution to protect the resident flock from any illness newcomers might bring with them. Then the five pigeons joined one of the coops, the parrot went to his new home with a friend with multiple parrots, and Snowball settled into a large cage in the living room.

Snowball was a mature white pigeon, and very comfortable with humans. She would settle easily on a chair arm for a visit, or land on an available shoulder or hand. She showed no signs of distress. She ate well, and listened to the sounds of the resident and wild birds without becoming agitated. She adapted quickly, coming out to fly several times a day and spending a good bit of time on the screened front porch, which is large and sunny, offering good flying space. She was safe and enjoyed a sort of freedom at the same time.

Bobby called each week to check on her. His stay in rehab was not going so well. Instead of two months, he might need three or more. I wasn't concerned until his voice began to sound strident. More and more, he argued that he needed the bird with him. He couldn't be comfortable without her. He wanted to send one of the nephews to pick her up even though he could no longer care for her, or even be around her.

The problem wasn't just that she couldn't stay with him in the rehab unit, which it turned out, would release him fairly soon. According to his doctors, bird dust would be harmful to

Bobby. Bird feathers create a kind of dust as the wings move and especially when new feathers come in. People with lung issues are usually quite sensitive to dust and it is a danger for them, particularly in a closed space. Bobby didn't care about the dust; he became more and more desperate to have Snowball back.

We were at a point of decision. As I thought about options, it began to occur to me to wonder what Snowball might think. In fact, I suddenly realized that Snowball was being treated like a toy, not as a living creature. Her person who was so devoted to her was sounding more and more like someone in a vampire novel, needing the life force of another to survive.

I felt confused about what was right. Beyond that, I began to wonder who was I in all this and what really was sanctuary for anyway? I paced about in the forest, muttering to myself that I had promised both to take care of the bird and to give the bird back. Of course that was before I realized the bird had a valid and independent life and was not simply Bobby's object. He of course would not describe her that way, I began to believe she might feel that way. I was getting alarmed – whose interests were more important, Bobby's or the bird's? I also felt sad, and foolish that I had not before considered the issue of the bird's nature, who she was, and what she would really want.

Nonetheless, I invited Bobby to visit Snowball at the Sanctuary as soon as he felt able. I talked to Snowball about it but who knows what I actually communicated. She went on flying cheerfully around the porch, and perched on my shoulder. I was worried.

Bobby and the nephew (a different one from those who brought the birds, and not scary at all) arrived early one sunny afternoon in July. I was startled. Bobby looked like Count Dracula straight from the tomb; he was pale, with long scraggly grey white hair, dressed completely in black with an oxygen tank in tow. His grey skin and shuffle gave a good imitation of a wraith.

We all went to the front porch to visit Snowball. The bird took one look at Bobby and flew away as far as she could get. Silence. I went and got her, brought her back and handed her to him. She flew off again, with much fluttering and ruffling of feathers. We went through several more efforts to get the two together when Bobby suddenly announced he was sure this was not Snowball.

Instead he went to the part of the porch closest to a pigeon coop and started calling "Snowball, Snowball" with his thin scraggly voice. No one answered. I had no idea what to do except to say that the bird on the porch really was Snowball and she must just be confused. The nephew said nothing, just looked from me to his uncle to the bird with dismay.

Finally I suggested that we look around a bit, let the bird settle down and then see what happened. I had begun to realize that the bird perfectly well realized who he was and wanted no part of him. Whatever relationship there had been seemed over for Snowball. Since this episode, I have seen pigeons remain connected to their humans even after long periods of separation, and reunite joyously. Like Snowball, they make their wishes clear. This was the first time I saw one reject a former companion. Faced with Snowball's choice, I was confused and upset and back to wondering what the right thing was to do.

When our tour was complete, Bobby confessed he had to return to another stint in rehab and so could not really accommodate the bird yet. Besides, he was now convinced this bird was not Snowball at all. In a sort of a way he was correct; she had moved on. So I volunteered that he should not worry, that Snowball was fine and he should just concentrate on getting well. They finally left. I collapsed on the porch with Snowball, who was back to her calm relaxed self.

Months passed. Bobby called less frequently, perhaps every 2 weeks or so, and we spoke very briefly. I let him know the bird was fine. Truth to tell, she was in fact flourishing, now cooing to the other birds in residence. I, however, was not fine. I was very worried about what would happen next and coming to the point of view that Snowball should be entitled to choose as well. If the bird rejected a person, she should not return with him as if she had no rights at all.

I was realizing that I had not quite recognized what now was clear; birds have her own lives and with that comes certain rights. The fact that Snowball was a bird and did not speak English did not mean she was an inanimate object. This awareness was a game changer. I was horrified to realize how short sighted I had been when I fostered birds previously, all without realizing it. Once I really saw her in this new light, I was quite impressed that she was undisturbed, while I was so upset. She had voted, knew she'd been heard, and apparently had decided all would be well. And she was right.

Bobby came out of rehab and went to his Bronx nephew to recuperate further. He called wanting to pick Snowball up and bring her "home." I suggested he wait and see how his health improved. I gently inquired what his doctors said about the dust problem. He announced that he didn't care about doctors. He just wanted his bird. I then spoke to the nephew who said his uncle was not recovered at all and he thought it was unwise for him to have any birds.

Finally it came to me that I had to be the voice for the bird. And that I should not have made a promise that had consequences I could not possibly understand. I must simply renege. I went out again and tramped around in the forest until I felt clear. Whatever anyone else thought, I knew what the bird wanted, and the bird got a vote just as well as everyone else, especially as it was her life.

Any relationship that is real has the potential for change; why not one between two different species? Perhaps those relationships require even more subtle care because of communication difficulties and apparent power differences. I had made my decision.

Armed with this new awareness, I called Bobby, and told him I did not think it served anyone for the bird to go where she clearly did not want to go and that Bobby could easily secure another companion animal from any number of shelters. I felt quite sad for Bobby, who wanted the old days back and understandably was upset at the loss of his friend. But I tried to help him see that this choice would serve everyone more completely. He did not agree.

I endured a month of frequent threatening phone calls, and so did the woman who had adopted Bobby's parrot. The only person not scared was Snowball. She was as calm and lovely as could be. As soon as I was completely convinced I had made the right choice, I introduced her into the coops so that she could again follow her nature and be a flock creature. Shortly thereafter she had a mate: a gorgeous large racing bird who was strong and very taken with her. Babies ensued. Life went on.

Eventually "lawyers"— bad imitations, I thought, of the real thing— were calling and threatening to sue. I said the bird had been moved because I was alarmed, and repeated that it was clear it was in no one's interest for Bobby and the bird to be reunited. After all, he refused to believe that bird even was Snowball. I went on to say that if I received any more calls, I was going to report the harassment to NY state troopers. There were no more calls.

I have pictures of Snowball and her first babies on the walls of my house. They show her as I knew her: sturdy, confident and clear about her right livelihood, as the Buddhists say. She wanted to be a bird with a bird life, and she succeeded. While she was about it she offered me a very great lesson; it is not just humans who have destinies and life paths. Mostly, humans just don't realize that. I am so grateful for this rich experience. It has permanently changed the lens through which I look and my world is so much richer for it.

Francis

CHAPTER 6

Francis had a hard beginning; he contracted PMV, the debilitating virus so common in the wild pigeon world. Usually the wild birds die unless somehow they get medication. As the medication is expensive and vets who will treat these birds are few, survival is rare.

As fate would have it, Francis was lucky. A woman who loved birds found him on the lower East Side in Manhattan, took him to her vet and he recovered. He then lived in her apartment, separated from her six or seven other pigeons for a several years. She thought it would be best to separate them to keep any disease at bay. She meant well, but didn't realize how important a flock was to a pigeon.

After some years she began to have lung difficulty. The dust from the birds in her apartment was always present. Her doctor insisted that the birds go. She was terribly upset to be parting with her adopted family, especially her favorite, Francis. I have seen any number of people get very close to the pigeons once they have been with them a bit, and it is always quite sad to let go, even when it is the best thing for both of them.

My pigeon rescue person in the city asked if I would take them, and I was pleased to welcome them. They arrived elegantly one afternoon in a big Lincoln Town Car, and happily began living on the glassed-in porch. There they got to be a flock of sorts and to fly about easily. There were logs for perching and other pigeons to get to know. It was great freedom after the apartment. Their joy was tangible; they were able to be pigeons after a long time of being pets, and they talked to one another cheerfully and constantly.

Francis was clearly the head bird. He had the best log. He was quiet and at ease in the new place, leading any new birds into the community. These birds had been near each other but not actually lived together closely for years; the new setting cleared that up and they began to be themselves. However, they were not young birds and they too had difficulty breathing easily. (Respiratory troubles are common to birds, especially when they had been long in close quarters.)

Their previous person, Mrs. Martin, came several times to visit them, just to be sure she had put them in the right place. And of course, she visited her favorite, Francis. He always seemed pleased to see her as well. For two years, the flock continued to thrive. Then one by one the other birds fell away. Their early rough living conditions shortened their lives. Their passing was gentle, with no struggle. They were just finished and departed one by one. Finally there was only Francis.

Francis and I started going into the garden under the trees to explore. He loved to be outside and we went where I did not think he was in any danger, below the big trees. One morning I was sitting on a stone bench under the magnolia tree when a big redtail hawk brushed my shoulder and dived for Francis. I shrieked and the hawk took off, but we were all very frightened. Francis was shuddering, very alarmed. We went into the house and sat together for a long time, until his fear melted. It was a near miss, and we never went there again.

Despite our good company together, I soon realized Francis would be lonely to be a single bird in a species that needs a flock. I had heard of another bird who was a young female and an inside bird, but whose person had died. I thought maybe she could do with a new home. The adopting family were delighted to hear she had a chance at a new life here.

She was indeed a lovely little pigeon and delighted to meet Francis. Both of them were glad for a new friend. We named her Sarah, and they settled into the porch together, until a few months later, all the birds went north to the Sanctuary for the summer. At the time all my house birds, a flock of cockatiels and the two pigeons, would go up to the Rhinebeck Sanctuary to enjoy a change of place. They lived in the country from summer through fall and then returned to the city.

Francis and I became quite close after the episode with the hawk. He was quite an intuitive bird and he certainly knew he had been in great danger. He began to come inside each evening to just hang about on my shoulder and purr. Pigeon purrs are not like a cat's; at first I did not recognize it as an expression of pleasure and kindness. When his relaxed purring became routine, I was delighted. As time went gently on we had an ever-deepening connection.

He remained cautious outside and did not go unless we went together. In his domestic shelter, he made quite a number of friends, people who held him softly, and got to know him in a way that opened their hearts. He was a favorite of our visitors.

Our easy friendship went on for about ten years. Then I could feel that he was just not as vibrant. We spent a lot of time together on the front porch, looking and listening as the evening settled in. And then one afternoon Francis came out and just stood by me; I picked him up and we sat together, enjoying each other. Looking back, we both knew that he would soon be leaving and he did not want it to be a surprise.

It was only six mornings later when Mike, the young man who tends the birds and lives in the red barn, came in and said, "I am so sorry; I think Francis is gone."

After two days to allow Sarah to adapt, we had his funeral in an honored place outside the greenhouse window with lots of flowers. His friendship was a great honor. It is not often one has such an opportunity to share a strong connection with another species. The experience itself is a shared language, unique to each bird. I suspect that is what is so wonderful.

After some time we thought Sarah should have other pigeon friends and we took her up to a coop of pigeons who had health challenges: a bad wing, a lost eye, a lost leg. They were fine, but just needed to safe shelter. She lived another year there and then she too was gone. I thought perhaps landing in a good flock was enough for her.

In all, he lived for about 28 years. And I think he would say he had gotten good results from his experiences. Certainly I found him an enormous gift in my world, and a great friend.

The Sanctuary
CHAPTER 8

As I got to know The Pidge I began to realize how exceptional she was.

After a difficult time and being thrown out of her flock when she was injured and very thin, she tried hard to escape my efforts to help her; apparently it was not easy to give in to the unknowns. She kept her distance for almost a year, in her place on the dining room table; then suddenly she changed her mind and appeared, flying though the living room.

That was the beginning of this adventure. And now I often ask, where could this miracle possibly have come from? And then, muttering, I just wander on through the birds and acres that fill our Sanctuary.

Sharing these stories, I realize that I was learning quiet and powerful lessons all along. Although it started with Pidge, my teachers were not only pigeons, but also chickens, turkeys and wild creatures. I was fortunate to find the old house surrounded by the forest; how completely magical it has been!

It took years of watching the world around the farmhouse to fall in love with the land. With the arrival of Pidge I began to understand what a blessing the opportunity was. Observing the habits of the creatures wandering by the big greenhouse window, I learned to see their world differently.

A bear came by from time to time; it took a bit to know that he just wanted seeds for a snack, not the chickens. Some humans working here were quite frightened about the bear dangers. I was also ready to defend the chickens no matter what. But then one day, the chickens saw the bear, got bored and wandered away, leaving him to his meal. I realized that I had misunderstood him. As long as I did not interfere, there would be no problem.

I began to see that the natural world was running on its own system. In fact, it was doing much better than we humans. We seem to be drifting further and further from connection with nature. I would never have paid attention either if it had not been for Pidge and the ongoing discovery of how interesting she was.

After Pidge died I wanted to celebrate her life. Giving homes to a few birds who needed them seemed a rightful way. So I started the Sanctuary in 2007 with two big coops for pigeons on the hill behind the house, and one coop next to the front porch. As more birds appeared I realized I'd created an organization, and now the Sanctuary is an official non-profit.

I never advertised or marketed the Sanctuary, but I did create a website so that people could find us, and know there was possibility for help for some birds. We continued to offer shelter and food to birds in need, although we are still not equipped for rehabilitate injured birds. We house and help a significant number of birds, but we cannot fix a broken wing. I hoped to do just that at first, but when someone brought an injured hawk I realized that creature needed more sophisticated help than we could provide. Besides, to rehabilitate live animals you must have the right license.

After a few years our bird population increased. We have begun to be very careful about taking in new citizens; it is not wise or helpful to be overwhelmed because overcrowding doesn't serve the birds or the Sanctuary. Now when someone contacts us with a domestic bird rescue, we carefully assess what we might do, often finding another home for the creatures.

We have several coops for pigeons: the original pigeon coops on the hill and the one by the house, a pigeon coop for birds who are handicapped in one way or another and need a home to be safe.

There is a designated pigeon coop for those who do not have homing instinct but fly easily. Without homing ability flying free is very dangerous; we have a big area to supply room for flight.

And finally, we created one in the recent pandemic when there were significant number of pigeons who needed new homes. Covid issues caused quite a bit of difficulty for some pigeon owners, so that space has been important for new arrivals.

There are also two chicken coops. The first shelters meat chickens, having been engineered to have big breasts and who are thought to have very short life spans. So far they have lived four or five years, but their flocks generally stay small.

The other is a flock of chickens who have come from here and there in need of a home. They are most beautiful and love to come out and then wander back to their place. They are not out all the time because hawks and other predators see them as dinner. During hawk migration we cannot let the chickens roam.

All of these coops are fortified, since wild creatures get hungry and are very smart. It is important for all the folks here to be closed up at night, the time of greatest danger. Very occasionally we will have an invasion, and must refortify.

Across the road, there is a pond with geese, and currently two young turkeys, fenced in but each enjoying a large space for wandering.

Finally we have of late had a poignant kind of work, a hospice of sorts. Sometimes a bird is not as sturdy as it initially seems, and begins to show signs of declining. We have discovered that birds understand when their time is nearly over. It is quite different from the human world in that respect.

Their departures seem elegant and for the most part timely, although we have mourned each death. These last moments seem to fit the creatures lives. And the hospice also serves to protect all the birds from occasional contagious diseases. Certainly the safety of the whole group is primary.

Another element of the Sanctuary is the forest and the land. Up beyond the coops, we have a stone circle of monolithic stones intended to honor the land and its beauty. The circle marks the entry to the forest, next to an area of naturally present boulders that contribute to the general peacefulness.

What started with finding the old farmhouse has made possible things that I would never have imagined. Each part has made the place seem more complete. And I feel very honored to have found this place and met these creatures.

BILLY

GERALD

LURKEY

PETEL

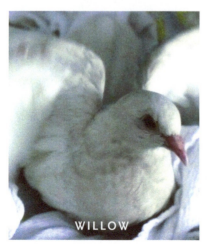

WILLOW

FRANCIS

Profiles: Stories of Remarkable Birds

As with any species, some individuals are more memorable than the rest. The profiles of the birds featured here are especially unique, deeply deserving of recognition. Most of these extraordinary folks have passed on now, leaving us with marvelous memories of them.

I have had close connection with each of the birds in this section. It's been a privilege to know them well and understand their lives. They each showed courage, determination and individuality. Each of these flock creatures have remarkable experiences and gifts.

It takes time and careful attention to actually understand the individuals, but of course that is true of our species as well. I got to know these birds as "people with feathers," each with his or her own path.

Their lives are shorter than human lives, but each one has meaning. Their lives and deaths touched me deeply. I trust you will enjoy getting to know these wonderful birds as part of discovering the wonder of the creatures flying through your world.

Reginald

CHAPTER 9

Reginald sat peacefully in his coop as he had done for most of his life. The wooden Amish shed is small, but comfortable in the cold windy weather; the floor is layered with fresh soft hay and the heat lamp takes the temperature up a few degrees in the 5-degree nights. He had spent all his days in our Sanctuary, exploring his pasture: digging for bugs, talking to the two hen turkeys who are his flock, a companionable little group chatting to each other all day and going easily into the coop at night. Now my good friend was dying but seemed calm.

Reg was a five-year-old bronze turkey who came with Sarah from a nearby farm to companion the already resident 6-month-old turkey, Lurky, a bronze hen turkey hatched out at the local farm store. The Sanctuary they joined included pigeons, chickens, doves, a few pheasants, geese and with their addition, a happy flock for our first turkey.

When Lurky first came she lived with the chickens, but she didn't bond with them, and started exploring the forest on her own. That was not a safe choice; she had no wild animal skills and could easily have been killed. Mike had to round her up daily. It soon became obvious that other arrangements had to be made or Lurky would not survive.

Next we introduced her to four geese in their pasture by the pond. That field is fenced to keep its inhabitants from wandering into the dirt road or the surrounding forest. Her new pasture was just across the road from the old farmhouse, the core of the Sanctuary, and easily observed from the big front porch.

At first, things seemed to go well. I went each day to just be with them. One morning the youngest goose climbed excitedly up in my lap. When she eventually got down, Lurky, after peering fixedly for a short intense time, jumped up, gazed trustingly at me, and settled for what felt like a long cozy visit.

I was lost in wonder and delight that this vulnerable little creature would take such a risk. She was so small and completely undefended. It turned into a daily ritual; I treasured our times together.

Turkeys seem ancient, quite akin to the dinosaurs I have seen in museums, with large feet, long neck, pointed beak and clear penetrating gaze. They seem much less flighty than the other birds I know well, the chickens and pigeons, the doves and of course the wild birds I still loved to observe. In our time together, Lurky was very focused and very still, at times looking out at the surroundings and others just staring up at me. I took it as an invitation to relationship.

When the geese, as geese will, pulled out some of Lurky's feathers to build their nests, I was heartbroken. Her adopted goose family had treated her like an object, and for her safety we had to separate them. The rest of her life she waited every day for the geese to come to the fence they shared so that they could visit. Just like humans who will return doggedly to a rejecting family, she seemed to hope that all could be as it once seemed.

I created a pen next to the geese's enclosure. (Whatever had happened, Lurky still loved her goose family, and I wanted her to be close enough to see them). Happily, her friendship with Reg was much more satisfying. She was devoted to him and he to her; in every sense of the word they shared a life.

The other turkey, Sarah, was tolerated, but never really part of their club. While not an outcast she was not very important in their daily relationship. She took to sitting behind the coop and near the fence, underlining her separation. The other two did not seem to mind. One day a fox dug under the fence near her, and made a quick dinner. Her death was a change in life in the pasture, but the bond between the other two continued as always; they still had each other.

Over the years, Lurky and I retained our early bond as well; she ran to the fence whenever she saw me. As her life continued she developed a cancerous tumor under a wing. Dr. Elaine Tucker, our excellent vet, presented treatment options of various intensity, and I chose the least invasive possible so that she could enjoy her remaining time. Dr. Tucker agreed. It seems most farm bred turkeys have 3–5-year life spans (unless they become dinner, the usual outcome).

When she got sick and came to the porch (which doubles as our hospital ward) she was trusting: no thrashing, no screaming and in general no complaining, though she did call to her flock in the pasture across the road. We were friends, and we both knew she needed some help.

But exactly what help we still had to decide. Lurky was already five; it seemed silly to cause her fear and suffering. Treatment would require her to leave home, and she would be with strangers. It would not extend her life and it would destroy her sense of security in her flock. A flock is a critical element in bird life; it parallels human community and the birds require their unique communities to flourish.

Over the summer it became more and more obvious that Lurky's health was failing. She had an increasingly vacant look even though she still came to the fence for treats and a visit. Day by day she slowed. I returned Lurky to the field with Reg when I could, bringing her into the porch infirmary when she needed a rest. In her last days Reg was always nearby.

I had checked on her on her at about noon, and she was quiet but alive, breathing easily and seemingly without distress. Two hours later she was gone. She died quietly by the fence with Reginald nearby. Reg slowly walked up and down, first close to her then farther away. He nudged her; she would not move.

We left her in the field with Reg for a few hours; then Mike took her body to the porch in a plastic bag while we decided where to put her grave. As soon as she was gone Reginald started frantically hunting: first the fence line, then the coop, then the fence line again. Finally, he stood near the coop crying loudly. The sound came from somewhere very deep, a wailing cry, something I had not heard before. It touched me deeply. We were both grieving our friend. I went to the field to be with him but there was no way out of it; our good companion was gone. He was wild with grief.

Reginald is a large bird and he seemed even bigger as he shrieked and paced over the field searching for Lurky. I sat with Reg for long times on the bench by the picnic table in his field. He would come, look at me and just cry out. He was so obviously distraught I thought he might die. He would sometimes allow me to give him a pat or a head scratch, but he soon went back to his frantic cries.

Five months passed before Reg calmed, but he never recovered from the loss. He sat on his hay in his home, distant and peaceful. He was not part of this life anymore. He observed the field and the three new little hen turkeys, but he didn't get involved.

Whenever I arrived he looked up and seemed pleased by the visit. He ruffled his feathers as I patted him and he turned his long neck, peering up with steady eyes. And then he settled again into his hay. I often brought him watermelon since I discovered some long time back how much turkeys like it. He pecked vigorously at the ripe pink melon. I fended off the other turkeys who tried to snatch his share because he was now too slow to defend it. Flock turkeys always seem to want what someone else has even though they have their own supply.

Death is so enormous, so far beyond language. This big turkey slowly became discernibly more tranquil as his body weakened. In a powerful way, we became closer as friends as he faded. I do not question his death. His timing seemed impeccable.

I miss him still. I could see his body was failing and he was not much present in this life. Yet I was so connected to him that his absence left a bittersweet hole.

I was so honored to be his close friend, and ultimately, student. Experiences like this gently remind me that change is the nature of life. But a close connection with these birds is worth any eventual loss, not a risk but a certainty. The good times are so rich and so shiny that sadness is a worthy price.

Jewelene, Petel & the World of Pigeons

CHAPTER 10

People have preconceived ideas. Remember that anyone or anything is a product of the environment where it lives. The preconceived ideas that people have about the pigeons reflect human biases and ignorance, not the world of the pigeons. As I discovered over and over, the Sanctuary's birds each have their own story and needs, as do the people who love them.

This story is about the friendship between Petel and Jewelene. With her partner Rey, Jewelene rescued Petel as a baby bird. Petel lived his entire life, 20 plus years, with Jewelene. Rey, her partner, died of AIDS when Petel was about 15, leaving the two companions to fend for themselves.

I learned of Petel and Jewelene when the pigeon rescue called to see if I would take the bird temporarily when Jewelene recovered from pneumonia. The pigeon had nowhere to go because Jewelene's family would not help. In fact, Jewelene told me later, the family planned to kill him if they had the opportunity. Later I discovered she was not exaggerating; they thought her companion Petel was at best an annoyance, at worst a burden.

During Petel's first visit, I learned how many medical issues Jewelene really had; she was HIV positive (though she did not have active AIDS), her health complicated by diabetes and heart difficulties. She also struggled with bipolar disorder, which she managed quite well with only occasional, as she said, 'bipolar moments.' In all, she managed these medical issues quite well, and had found good doctors at Mt. Sinai who would help her. She had a remarkable ability to find her way in the medical world. I never heard her complain.

Because of her unexpected hospitalizations and housing challenges, I began to take care of Petel more frequently. I developed so much respect for Jewelene's ability to manage a difficult life, so I just went along with what was needed. Often I would get a call to take him for a few days, sometimes for weeks. He was always well behaved and friendly.

Throughout these interruptions — moving house, medical events, her family's refusal to take care of Petel — she would bring him to the Westchester house I had then, visit when she could, and pick him up eagerly at the end of his time away. The love between them was palpable, and she was delighted to see that he was thriving. He was clearly just as pleased to see her.

I remember the first time she came to the house. She wanted to give me money for taking care of him. She said she didn't have much but she could give me four dollars, if that would be

OK. Of course it was, and we would spend some at McDonald's so she'd have lunch for her train ride back to the city.

At one point she told me it was vital for her escape the cold northern winter, and bring Petel to Florida. She had lived on the street in lower Manhattan for several years, and it just was too hard. She was convinced that warmer weather would help. As it turned out I had extra air miles, and off we went to LaGuardia, hopefully to send them both on to Florida.

As we approached the airport I suddenly got very nervous about trying to get Petel safely on and off the plane. But at the ticket desk, we shared their story with the airline representative, emphasizing how important the bird was. I shared my worry that she might get through the gate but have to give up the bird, and we had to be sure that wouldn't happen.

There was a slight pause, and then he said, "Don't you worry; I will walk her to the door and all will go well."

I was so stunned I stopped breathing for a bit, and then sat down to contemplate. It seemed a miracle had happened.

However, the Florida relocation did not go as well as expected, and after about two months I heard from her mother. "They found Jewelene on the street in a diabetic coma. I don't know if I should pick her up or not. You know, Petel was standing on her, or no one would have noticed."

I was surprised, but soon she explained that Jewelene's stepfather was not only uninterested in the bird but also very careful with his money.

I asked, "How will you feel if she dies alone, just guarded by the bird? Then what?"

Her mother decided to go to Florida and brought Jewelene and Petel back safely. It was a near miss.

Later I decided that Florida was an old dream for Jewelene, and it didn't turn out how she'd imagined. She was sad and most worn out when they returned. And neither her family nor her potential landlords would take the bird. She had to recover from the Florida events and so needed comfort and ease. She found somewhere to live, but it was away from medical help and quite a distance from my house and thus the bird, who had come back to stay with me while she settled in. We planned visits every two weeks or so.

That was the beginning of dialysis and more physical difficulty. But she was getting well enough to look for a place in New York again and she did manage to find an apartment. It was a good long subway ride to the city to get to the hospital, but at least it was possible. She always had a future plan, and hoped she'd found the stability she wanted.

All she really wanted was a simple life, but it was hard to maintain and she was getting tired. I admired her efforts greatly and often thought what an enormous help Petel had been in her life. It was a true hardship not to have him with her. And the return to New York should have made life better for both of them.

Jewelene was determined to have a good life with Petel, no matter what happened. During these last days, finally in a respectable hospital, she needed extra food to ease her diabetes. She asked the nurse, who replied, "I do not have time to bother with that." It was apparently the last straw, as Jewelene pulled out the various needles, walked out, and took the subway for two hours to her place. Two days later she was dead. It was one unkindness too many, and she was done.

Fortunately I had the bird safe with me, though of course he lost his great friend. And he and I sat for a long time, while I talked about her and how excellent she was even when she faced difficult times. He was quiet, but did not seem bedraggled. And then he moved on, just resting and taking in the sights from the porch and appearing for a snuggle in the living room now and then.

Petel had lived on the street with her when she was homeless. When they took shelter in The Twin Towers the night before 9/11, he was there. In fact, Petel was the reason she and her partner were not killed; they had traveled uptown to get bird food because it was much cheaper. Petel tried it, threw up two or three times, and so delayed their return. They missed the explosions and the toxic debris. In all my bird experience I have never seen a bird throw up. So it surely was a blessing that he picked this moment, and it has never seemed to me to be an accident.

Of everyone I have met in this work, I appreciate Jewelene and Petel most. Their love and care for each other was endless, and she never put him in danger. He was a completely reliable companion and she lived longer and more comfortably with him. She and I had a relationship for more than 7 years. I was most honored that when she departed Petel stayed with me another year and a half, just resting up. Surely he earned it.

In all, I found the two of them understood each other so well that their endings seemed appropriate and rightful. He waited for her to go, rested and then went to meet her in the next life. I will forget neither of them. Ever.

Rob

CHAPTER 11

Rob, a strong black Cochin rooster, came from a suburban town which did not like roosters. The original folks with whom he was born loved him dearly and were worried the town would take him away. As a last resort they brought him to the Sanctuary. We had several roosters and only took him because he needed a place as there is often trouble between roosters.

He was gentle, big and wisely created a subordinate place with the older rooster who led the flock. After a year he had become part of the group and seemed to fit in easily, following along with the hens as they came out to forage. The hens loved digging about, capturing abundant bugs and worms, and a good time was had. I watched him carefully as I did not want him to wander off into the forest where he might easily get lost or attacked.

Rob could be seen strutting across the chicken yard on guard when they all went out into the yard. The chickens followed the roosters back in as evening came, since they seem to know night is not a safe place for them. The night is when the predators come. However we had not had trouble for a long time as we had taken care to fortify every coop.

Nonetheless, a new menace had arrived recently: a mink. Minks are very smart and extremely dangerous, eating any living thing they find. This mink tunneled under two extended feet of wire to get into the coop, and now there was a lot of prey available for him, unknown to us.

Suddenly Mike, who takes good care of the pigeon flock and our coops, came running to the house, shouting. There were eight dead pigeons, three dead pheasants, and Rob did not look good. We were shocked because we imagined we were well secured. But we had never experienced a truly determined mink. We hurried back to the coops to be sure there was no other deaths.

But there was a shock for us all. Rob was still standing but looked frozen. He was utterly still and very quiet. Both Mike and I saw that something was very wrong. We immediately found a huge gash across the back of his neck, with a lot of blood steadily dripping. Rob had stopped the mink from getting near his flock or they surely would have been killed. He had evidently paid a big price.

At once I wrapped him in a towel and rushed him to the vet, who gave him oxygen and pain meds. She commented gently that these were extremely serious injuries and sadly gave us the news that we would have a hard time keeping him alive.

We wanted the very best possible next steps for him so we brought him home and started hand feeding him. Day after day he seemed to get better. He was breathing easily and standing up on his own. We were cautiously optimistic. We created a big place on the front porch where he could walk about and have a bed of leaves and eat a bit if he wanted.

Rob had defended his new home vigorously, driven off an extremely powerful predator and managed to stay alive himself. The mink must have paid a serious cost as well, since there were no other invasions at night after the assault. We could have easily lost more animals had Rob not made such an enormous effort.

Just in case, we put out have-a-heart traps with chicken livers with the thought of catching the mink to rehome him somewhere. For ten days we reset the traps. But the wild kingdom has a way of getting the news out, and they must have heard our place was dangerous because the chicken livers were never eaten.

We went on hand feeding Rob, who ate patiently, and pushed his porch leaves into something of a nest. His healing seemed to be moving slowly forward. He walked about and made contented gurgling sounds. We were pleased at his progress and patience, allowing us to feed and comfort him two or three times each day. After about two weeks, we thought he was doing quite well. One afternoon, we went to the porch at five to check on him, and indeed there he was walking about looking sturdy.

At six, Mike came in and said, "He is gone."

I thought he meant off the porch. But no... Rob was dead. The two of us who had just seen him were completely shocked. I insisted that he be brought in so we could be sure. In fact, our wonderful rooster was just gone, after a heroic struggle.

I had been so close to him, and so proud; I could not understand why he left. Finally I realized I had seen this happen before. Birds do not seem to accept injuries in general. This bird in particular was so alive that these injuries were a big shock to his system. He seemed to accept life could not be the same. And he was so easily gone. When I called the vet to tell her, she was not surprised, saying she thought he had made a wise choice.

By this time I have seen a number of passings, and I have realized that these creatures have understanding that we do not. Most likely they are just ready, and therefore let go more easily than we understand.

I admired Rob very much for his heroism and for his ability to adapt to a new place, settling in to defend his new home and flock. He had time to recover and be treated with great gentleness as he considered the next stage. What a privilege it was to know him and to provide at some comfort at the end. We remember him as he was: a great addition to our Sanctuary flock and a splendid soul.

EXPLORING THE MAGICAL WORLD OF BIRDS

Billy

CHAPTER 12

Billy was not a young pigeon when he collapsed and nearly died on the steps of a Manhattan brownstone. He had injured a wing, could not move, and the future looked dim. However, a good Samaritan appeared, picked him up, gave him water and took him to a rehabber.

The rehabber was wonderfully talented and determined, working with Billy gently for over a year. She managed to bring the wing back in to usefulness and to restore Billy's energy. When her work was done she and the good Samaritan brought him to our Sanctuary.

When he first came, he looked about apprehensively. He was a wild bird not used to captivity despite his experiences of the last year. The Sanctuary was unknown territory. We waited to send him to a coop because we thought it would be better for him to recover completely. From the beginning he appeared interested in other birds.

When he had substantially recovered from his injuries, he was handsome and easy going. As bad luck would have it, in the coop, the first lady he was interested in did not share his passion. In fact, she was shrill and mean. But the next lady who appeared took to him promptly. Soon they retired to the front porch to enjoy life. And indeed they did! The porch is large and has a view of trees, the pond and other bird coops. Most of the birds feel secure there, so it is a good launching pad for newcomers.

In a short time these two were sitting on eggs and clearly delighted with each other. He seemed very pleased with his mate and most excited to see their baby.

All went along gloriously; the two were tending to the baby who had by now grown quite a bit and was starting to fly. Uncrowded and content, they had become a joyous family. Mike, who has enormous bird experience and tends the coops, declared his recovery a triumph. We were so pleased for them, especially after Billy's near-death experience.

One ordinary day I went to do an errand or two, and when I came back I went to the porch to see what was happening. I was shocked and heartbroken when I saw a black bird on the floor, clearly dead. He was still warm and showed no sign of wounds, but he was clearly gone. I absolutely did not want to acknowledge that it was Billy. I went in the house hoping Mike would tell me it was someone else, but he couldn't. It was a sad end for Billy's difficult road, so soon after he had settled in.

We soon decided that he had been bullied by a larger bird who apparently could not bear the good fortune of the little group. The baby and the mom were okay; they were terrified and shuddering, but not dead. She was badly shaken, looking wildly from side to side – searching for Billy and no doubt, the bully.

I picked her up to calm her, offered some Rescue Remedy (a calming homeopathic, useful because works gently and is not a drug) and soothed her. There was a section of the porch enclosed by screen and a door, so was not open to prowlers. We promptly put her on a high shelf perch with the baby in our screened in porch, with water and food and left them to settle quietly, we hoped.

I showed Billy's body to his lady and the baby so there was no confusion, and we sat sadly down to take in what had happened. There was little to say, but we stayed with Billy for some time until twilight. Then we wrapped him in a nice towel, getting ready for the funeral. We have found these rituals create comforting closure. And we surely needed closure here.

In the evening of the murder we called our excellent animal communicator; she can often know and feel things from the creatures that we do not. Often her understanding removes much of the immediate sorrow that darkens a loss. She told us that Billy had always wanted a family, and he was happy to fight to the end to protect what he had desired for so long.

The rest of the family slowly recovered, and we saw to it that they always had food, water, and safety. After several months they seemed strong enough to join another coop and a new flock. They have done well since.

And Billy? He too is complete. It was a long hard way from the brownstone step to his family, but he finally made a home. We appreciated the extraordinary efforts he made, to recover and then to partner and protect his mate and hatchling. He surely was a great example of why I created the Sanctuary.

EXPLORING THE MAGICAL WORLD OF BIRDS

Roost II: Passing

CHAPTER 13

Roost and his ladies continued to wander the Sanctuary grounds for years, eating ticks and other bugs, and returning to the aviary at night. The farmhouse now had what it had in its early years – a flock of chickens at home on the farm. I sat on the porch in the twilight and basked in our good fortune.

We spent several years in this fine fashion; more hens came and finally a chick hatched who turned out to be a carbon copy of Roost, beautiful with long feathers of mottled gold down his neck and over his back and a large arching tail of shimmering green black. All seemed to go well, with the senior Roost as the alpha male and Riley, as we called the son, a part of the flock. The expanding group was a bit hard on my gardening efforts as their favorite sites were generally wherever I planted new seeds, with soft earth where could dig and cluck excitedly to each other.

But there were nice eggs for breakfast, though the free ranging meant that many were laid under bushes and never found. The hens loved to scratch under the bird feeders by the greenhouse room and then peer in the living room windows intently as if whatever was inside the room was a kind of television. It must have been interesting for them as they came every day to discuss our habits among themselves. It was completely satisfying to watch them and to join in their easy ways. In all, it was a very fulfilling and comfortable time of everything feeling as if what should happen had come to pass.

Then one warm afternoon in an early November I came home from doing errands to find Roost crumpled on the lawn by the driveway and only one hen, his favorite, still outside the coop. He was not moving.

The rooster had never ever been still in the time I had known him and certainly had never sat down in the open. A large red tail hawk sat in the birch tree twenty or so feet away. At first I thought Roost was dead, I walked quietly toward him; he rustled his wings and staggered a few feet under the nearby lilacs and then collapsed on the ground. I watched for several minutes trying to decide what to do. The hawk had not moved and was watching; I did not want to scare Roost into the open, making him even more vulnerable, but I wanted desperately to see if he was injured.

After what seemed like a very long time and was really only a few minutes, someone stopped by. Together we managed to capture Roost with a big bird net I have for emergencies. Roost was very frightened, breathing in shallow rapid rasps. I was so relieved to find he was not bleeding and not dead that at last I started breathing again after the shock. I wrapped him in a towel and took him home to the coop, where the others in the flock had already gone. Once there, he began to drink and climbed on a perch. I closed the doors, thanked providence that I had come home when needed and went in for the evening myself.

Roost spent the next few days resting in the coop. He was eating and drinking, always a good sign, but did not seem vibrant. Richie (who also helps me take care of the birds) said he thought Roost had a respiratory problem and we should give him a suitable antibiotic. After a few days, he seemed to progress nicely.

By this time, perhaps two years, Riley was in his prime, and was strutting quite proudly for the hens (eleven of them). He seemed more dominant now as he dashed through the hens, rounding them up as I had seen Roost do so often. Roost didn't look like the proud leader he had been; instead he sat on the perch with his favorite hen and watched from a distance.

I've often seen birds who become sad or badly disturbed fail quite quickly. It is always better if the old routine can reassert itself. I loved Roost deeply and admired his way of being the leader of his flock, carefully tending the hens and his son, making sure he alerted everyone if he found a particularly tasty batch of bugs. His robust cries would summon the rest of the flock and so everyone got to eat. He was a rich example of a creature living his nature completely. I was anxious for him to return to his old self, if possible, and so I was letting them all out together again. I hadn't seen the hawk for several days and it seemed safe.

It was now early December and getting chilly. Soon winter would lock in the cold, with its clouds and darkness and short days. The day of the next event I came out about four, it was getting dark and all the hens and Riley were in. Roost was in the driveway behind the house, wandering aimlessly. He would head toward the coop for a few feet then turn aside and just stand. All his old certainty and presence seemed to have dissipated; he seemed old and frail to me. I laid bits of corn toward the coop and after an hour, got him in. I was cold, exhausted and heartsick. Finally I just sat on a rock and cried. My friend seemed to be fading and the world would never be as it had been.

At first I thought I was making some mistake because I felt the loss so keenly, but finally I concluded that the loss was real and a big presence leaves a big hole and that is just how it is. Better to honor the relationship by feeling the grief than by papering it over with some manufactured "Ah well, it's inevitable, isn't it?" However true it may be, it's not a comfort. I have decided to just let myself mourn when someone I have loved leaves. And that loss seemed imminent with Roost.

One day I didn't see him; when I went to look I found him in the coop wedged behind nest boxes and covered in blood. He had been attacked quite viciously, apparently by his son. Birds will attack whoever is weakest in the flock. The pigeons do it and now I discovered what other chicken people knew; hens and roosters do too. This behavior safeguards the flock and avoids attracting predators, bird experts say. It makes a kind of sense, actually, because the old order is pushed out and the life of the flock continues.

I might have left Roost to the course of nature, I suppose, but I could not. I was heartsick. I got him out from the place he had chosen to hide, wrapped him up in an old towel, called the vet who treats farm creatures, and said I had an emergency. There was blood everywhere: dripping from Roost's wounds, on the floor, on my hands and clothes. I didn't care. I gave him a squirt or two of water to drink as I thought it would stabilize him a bit, and it did. I thought he couldn't have been stuck in the coop too long because he was still bleeding freely; the wounds had not clotted. I had heard no disturbance but then I had been planting some new trees farther away on the land. At least he was alive, the vet's office was open, and help was available.

The vet was a lovely, kind man, his office about 20 minutes over country roads. It seemed a long way that day. We determined that Roost should be hospitalized, kept warm and given various restorative drugs. A very bedraggled Roost spent five or six days there, with me visiting him so that he would know he had a link to home. He seemed glad to see me each time and perked up after I held him for ten minutes or so. I had not before had the experience of hugging a rooster, but it certainly is a profound communion; the rooster has big spurs and could do damage if he chose, or could tear a hole with his beak. Instead, each time he settled quietly into my arms and we just were together in the peace of the moment.

After five days, the vet suggested Roost was not progressing and perhaps we should end his life. I sat a moment and decided, "Well, I think I will bring him home and let him choose when to die. I don't think we are done, and unless he is suffering terribly, I think the choice is his." The vet gave me a supply of antibiotics with instructions and sent us off for whatever happened next.

Roost came into the house because it was now deep winter, 15 degrees outside. He lived in a canvas dog crate with screen sides and front so that he was contained but could see his surroundings and people he knew. He seemed listless. We gave him antibiotics with a dropper three times a day and offered dishes of his favorite foods: lettuce, dove seed and chicken mix.

Miraculously, after two days he was better. He held his head high, and gave a strangled crow, but a crow nonetheless. I had begun trying to accept his coming death; I was earnestly nursing him but without much hope. When I saw vitality begin to return I was completely joyous – my friend might stay! Soon he was strutting around the kitchen much as he had strutted around the yard, head held high, tail flourished, and beautiful golden collar feathers quivering with movement. We went on like this for about two weeks.

He seemed so much better that he began to act confined in the kitchen. He needed to be outside on some familiar surface, not a stone floor. We covered an outside coop with a dirt floor in thick plastic to cut off the wind, setting up food and water to entertain him for a day. The sun was shining and he was delighted to be on the earth; he scratched and dug and pecked as he had before. Since it was very cold and snowy outside, he came in that evening exhausted. He ate well and then fell deeply but comfortably asleep.

While he was living in the kitchen hospital I had been giving him hugs each day and in general providing company. At one point he eyed the white couch and just stood in front of it staring. Finally I realized he wanted to perch on it for the night. Out came the old sheets and up went Roost, who went right to sleep with a contented gurgle. It felt wonderful to be able to give him what he obviously wanted. I don't know what place in me it healed, but I could feel some very old sorrow melting as I looked at the nestled bird.

After several days of the morning journey to the outside coop with its dirt floor and an evening return to warmth, Roost became unusually quiet, indrawn. After two days, he stopped eating. That is what animals do when they are ready to leave. The great gift of this shared time had been that I realized in some deep way that his life and so his death belonged to him. I could support him, make him comfortable and hope he would stay, but the choice was not mine to make. The vet's wish to end his life some three weeks earlier had been invasive, and I knew now his timing was his own. Heroic treks to the best medicine around would honor my wishes, not Roost's.

One clear cold night in January, Roost and I watched a Harry Potter movie for a couple of hours. He sat in my lap with contented peacefulness. Finally I wished him goodnight, gave him an extra hug, thanked him for choosing my place and said I would be glad to see him the next day, but whatever he chose was fine. I went up to bed. He was gone in the morning.

In reflection, I felt his great peacefulness through the last part of his life. In his prime, he was a model of vibrant life; then he let go of that life naturally and comfortably. He always seemed to be himself, never in doubt and obviously clear about what rightful roosters do: guarding and leading the flock to find food and safety. He had done that in an impeccable way. The flock had peacefully followed his guidance, flourishing in the process. And then he was done.

Over my many years with animals I have been part of a lot of death and each time I feel honored to be able to be allowed to participate in such a momentous event as the departure of a soul from his earthly lifetime. The books I have read on human death and dying celebrate the approach and moment of death as one of the most sacred moments we experience.

Animals show us their wisdom in this way. As their bodies become weaker the creatures seem more and more peaceful; I have always felt the spirit was more present though the body was used up. What a privilege to share such a time with someone you care about. This rooster had chosen my place as his sanctuary and we had shared such good times. I was so grateful for the front row seat at the chicken pageant.

SANCTUARY

Willow

CHAPTER 14

Willow was a beautiful soul, who always lived as if she floated way above her difficulties, which generally troubled us, her human companions, more than they ever troubled her.

I met Willow at my vet's office, where I picked her up for the Sanctuary. The vet, well-known in our area, speculated that Willow was not yet walking but soon would be. As it turns out, Willow never walked at all, although for a time she did fly. She was always startlingly beautiful, completely alert and interested in her surroundings.

From the outset she was quite determined to have a good life, and was quite strong willed, letting us know what she liked and did not like in no uncertain terms. She particularly liked observing the world around her. When we realized she would not walk, we put her in a well-padded bed on the dining room table where we could see her and she could see us.

At first she studied her surroundings, getting to know the room, and looking out the big greenhouse window into the garden outside. The garden was home to all the wild birds, chipmunks and numerous squirrels. As winter came, she watched the deer come by as well. She always seemed interested and very peaceful.

Soon she began to befriend me and wanted to be helpful when I worked at the table. She would cling to my shoulder and purr, the most wonderful vibration of pleasure and contentment. I was enchanted to be chosen by this fascinating creature who never ever complained and was consistently paying attention from her perch.

One morning, Mike, who tends the birds carefully, called up to the second floor that there was an emergency with Willow. Apparently, she had jumped down from the table to the wooden floor and scooted along on her belly feathers to investigate the living and dining rooms. Although she seemed calm enough, we were appalled to see tracks of blood wherever she had explored.

I was quite shaken and watched her for a good while before I picked her up. She purred peacefully and seemed untroubled. She seemed a little miffed at first, but in no pain. I think she wanted to continue mapping the room. She was on a mission! Nonetheless, we brought her immediately to the vet.

He glared at me for being so careless with this gorgeous creature – but couldn't find an actual wound to explain the blood, which remained mysterious. Willow herself was calm, but we were terribly worried there had been some internal wound or injury.

Over the next few watchful days, the only one who was not troubled was Willow. She was calm at the vet's place and with the car rides back and forth. She was peaceful when we got back to the house and settled back into home base. As always, our concerns about her injuries, her disabilities, and her health were never reflected in her attitude towards the world, and never lessened her curiosity and calm. The disabilities never mattered to her.

And that was her greatness; she could not do ordinary pigeon world things, but she had a life she deeply enjoyed, and a human flock. When I realized how emotionally strong she was, it seemed sad not to be able to help her further, to see if she could be more mobile and comfortable.

We made many trips to NY City and our specialist vet. He was enchanted with her as well. He suggested calming drugs to limit her scooting, and other ways to keep her healthy, yet Willow never seemed to need the extra help, in her own way untouched by the meds, well settled and not disturbed by the absence of the usual pigeon possibilities.

The more we were with her the more magical she seemed. She had no sadness, no restlessness, and maintained an active interest in her daily life. The more I experienced her purring, the closer I felt to her. I was greatly honored by her trust and her ability to enjoy the small changes and comforts of our home pigeon Sanctuary.

After three years of a comfortable routine, I took a trek to St. John in the Caribbean, and left Mike to care for her. Three days into my vacation, the phone rang; Mike was completely distraught because Willow had suddenly died, with no evidence of injury or illness.

He thought it was his fault for some imaginary lapse in care. I thought it was my fault for leaving her. Even the animal communicator who knew her well and was connecting to her in my absence was distraught, saying "This cannot be! I just talked with her this morning, and she was fine!"

All her people were devastated, even visitors who had met her, but did not know her well. Many people have never met a bird up close and truly she was one of a kind. She was radiant, beautiful and interested, immediately engaging, and always present in a way I've seen with few creatures, people included.

I have learned that sometimes these people with feathers teach us quiet lessons with their deaths, which mark a point where they seem to complete their lives, simply being done, and content to be so. With Willow, once I recovered from the guilt and drama I was generating around her passing, I understood that she had not only had a good life, but had probably completed her adventure. Certainly, she let go with more grace than we let go of her.

She wanted to be here, and stayed for as long as was right, and when she was ready, she left. I admired her ease in life, her generous friendship, and came to respect and value her gentle passing as well. We missed her then and we miss her now, but we have never forgotten our time together.

Nelly

CHAPTER 15

Nelly was a small black pigeon from Brooklyn who had been injured before we met her. Her people could no longer of take care of her because their children were careless with their "pet" and she could not easily escape their games because she could not use her legs.

When she arrived, she seemed quite frightened and at once took up living under the television, her chosen safety zone. Treats, cajoling, and gentle offers of friendship didn't seem to help. Nothing seemed to persuade her to explore. Apparently, most of her life up to her arrival at the Sanctuary had made her feel unsafe, so we decided to allow her to create her own little sanctuary in our home. At night she returned into her own sleeping cage with food and water. Eventually, she was equally comfortable there.

This routine, unchanged, continued for about three years, when somehow she was cut in her crop (the soft tissue under the beak), and needed a trip to the vet at once. Neither the vet nor I could discover what had caused this, but it was most dangerous injury, one that often resulted in death for pigeons.

At the vet's office, we encountered a loudly howling beagle and a cat crying wildly. I saw that Nelly was very frightened, with all her 'under the television' comfort gone. I picked her up, told her she was safe and that we would make sure she was returned to her sanctuary. (I was not sure that talking to her in English had much purpose, but it was the only thing that came to mind.) She snuggled into my shoulder, relaxing despite the howling dog and the frightened cat, who continued their protests.

Dr. Tucker, our always gentle vet, called us in to patch up the wound, provided some pain meds and announced that the bird should now be well. Nelly was a bit tentative during the examination, but back in my arms, started to purr peacefully. She seemed exhausted but quiet.

When we got home and I started to put her down she pushed deeper into my arms. So we sat together for a bit. I tried again to set her in her sleeping place so she could rest, but again, she wanted to stay. In all the time we had known her she had not shown such affection. I called Dr. Tucker to ask what had changed, and she suggested that for the first time in her life Nelly had truly felt safe and comfortable, a life changing event for a bird who had been frightened for so long in her early life. What seemed to me a small kindness opened a door that she had always needed but never had. It came to be that we spent quite a bit of time together, and often she went gently to sleep against my shoulder. I felt most honored and enjoyed our connection.

It was devastating to Mike and me when, several months later, she accidentally collided with the leg of a couch, having scuttled too rapidly across the floor. Again, she had a serious cut that bled profusely, and nothing he could do to stop the bleeding worked. She died in Mike's hands.

Of course, both he and I thought that we had failed her, and that we should have been able to prevent the injury, or at least get her to the vet on time. But both the vet and our animal communicator reminded us that the accident wasn't a tragedy – in fact it was, oddly, a gift, a sign of completion. She had found peace in her life. Achieving this feeling of real safety meant that she had come home. And so, for her to die in the playground where she felt good wasn't such a bad thing.

It's ironic, how humans mourn what these creatures easily embrace. We imagined we were in charge, so we tried to save her and couldn't, wanting to fight fate. Over the years, I have come to believe that every being gets to choose their death – not in any suicidal way but through acceptance and understanding of the natural end of their life path.

She was quite a teacher to us. She had simple needs for safety and comfort, had finally gotten them fulfilled, and was at peace. We gradually accepted that she knew more than we did and we should honor her departure as her natural path, not as our failure. How little we knew about the hardships of her life before the Sanctuary, and the challenge of having legs that didn't work. We realized she was free. Her life taught us the benefit of accepting the gift of what we need most now, welcome and temporary, without conditions.

Gerald

CHAPTER 16

Gerald arrived at the house one day with a young man who had encountered him in the Bronx. He and his girlfriend had met the bird on the street and he did not seem able to fly, but they were able to pick him up. The rescuer said that they knew nothing of birds, but wanted this one to have a home. I accepted immediately.

Gerald is a large white pigeon, unusually beautiful and very interested in people. I supplied him with a nice cage with food and water, and the young man thanked me profusely, said goodbye to the bird, and disappeared. It was the beginning of a most interesting journey.

Gerald seemed in good health and humor and despite first impressions, quite able to fly. In fact he immediately flew about the living room a bit and then landed on my head. It was clear that he must have had a considerable experience with humans. He looked around alertly, found his favorite perches, and settled in, occasionally pecking on some seeds in the cage.

I have never experienced a bird so adapted to people. He clearly expected to stay and be treated well. He was immediately present, demanding to be seen and appreciated. Once he had defined his territory, he walked around a bit, flew through the kitchen and this time, settled for an extended perch on my head. I put him on my chair arm and he just stood there, as if he had always lived at the Sanctuary. Indeed, his attention to detail was fascinating, and he continues to be aware of small and large changes in our environment.

He has turned out to be smart, determined to do whatever he wants to do, whenever he wants to do it. He definitely wants to be the top pigeon in the house. Several days after he arrived, he attacked a lovely pigeon statue, apparently thinking it was competition. (He did seem surprised when the stone bird did not fight back.) After that we were more careful about closing doors to protect the art, but we were so intrigued with him that we forgave the statue and a few other pieces that went south as he investigated.

It did not take long for us to adjust to him or him to adjust to us and to other people who came. In fact, he promptly became the star of the Sanctuary. Most people have not had close experiences with birds and are surprised they are so taken with this beautiful and friendly creature. He flies back and forth between perches while watching the person and eventually lands on their heads or settles near them for a pet. Most people who meet him are as charmed as we were. (Of course it can be hard on balder folks, as pigeon feet are a bit claw-like, but he is remarkably gentle once he settles in.)

Once in a great while someone gets scared when he approaches. People who have little knowledge of birds can become quite alarmed. Birds are not like dogs or other mammals. Although as a rule they live in large flocks, they are quite individual. Opportunities to know a bird well are not often available, and so Gerald is an excellent ambassador.

Last year, a person came to visit who was most charmed with him and he with her. He sat on the couch just behind her shoulder, and periodically would groom a strand of her hair, or settle on her head for a scritch. All round both of them had a good time; Gerald was her first pigeon friend. Unfortunately she finally had to go home, but comes back regularly, largely, I think, because their relationship gives her so much delight. Gerald always greets her with enthusiasm, and their strong connection is getting stronger over time.

Gerald has been at the Sanctuary for over a year now and shows no sign of wanting to join other pigeons. He is charismatic and most unusual in that he is interested in his surroundings but not interested in others of his kind. Since there are a large number of elegant pigeons here, he could easily pick a flock and join it. I don't know what happened in his early life to create his preference, but it has created considerable pleasure for the human flock he's chosen as companions.

Occasionally, he interacts with the birds in his territory. One very young bird, Willie, consistently tries to get Gerald's seeds. At first Gerald jumped on the little one, but then he seemed to realize there was no real danger to his stash, so he backed off.

Depending on the season, Gerald spends a lot of time in what we call "camp," the front screened porch where he has flying space and six other birds nearby behind their own screen. It is his own space, and he seems most pleased with it.

In all, I am delighted the gentleman who found him brought him to us. He fits in easily and has shown many visitors that a bird is not a strange object or an alien creature, but a charming companion. That is sometimes a considerable accomplishment, seemingly effortless because of his curiosity and charm.

Gerald's routine rarely changes. He goes to "camp" after a breakfast of seeds and a look see so he will know if anything has happened in his surroundings. Once he is satisfied that all is in good order, he heads for his refuge, where he can see the outside world, and returns cheerfully for dinner at about seven. He shares space with two other pigeons: Millie, a bird who was afflicted by the PMV virus and so has neurological damage but is most pleased to be in a safe home, and Willy, the seed pirate.

By now, Gerald rules the house pigeon world, more kingly every day. What a great thing to have such pigeon royalty completely at ease, pleased with his world. Of course we are quite pleased as well and would welcome any other pigeons who could easily teach the wonder of the pigeon to humans unaware of what they're missing.

Conclusion

*"A bird does not sing because it has an answer,
it sings because it has a song."*

—Maya Angelou

I wrote this book to share the lessons from the birds and the potent introduction they offered to the natural world. I love the ease of these creatures in the cycles of life, season to season.

Most of the birds who have come to the Sanctuary needed a new home, or a place to stay for a time. It is truly a pleasure to provide that and to watch them get comfortable in a completely new place. They all adjust far more easily than I would have in the same circumstance.

I hope these portraits open new ways for you to discover the gifts of birds. The more you get to know them, the more you'll see their beauty. Of course, once you have had a chance to experience a relationship with an individual bird, your understanding of their gifts will open even more.

Birds like Pidge, Roost, Snowball and Reg have changed the way I know the world and myself. My relationships with the birds brought me step by step to the Sanctuary, an unexpected and wonderful journey. I hope these stories inspire you to find our way to your own journey with birds.

Support Us

We need your help! We hope you'll make a donation to sustain the Stonehouse Wood Sanctuary.

https://stonehousewoodsanctuary.org

We regularly accept new birds and advise folks about rescuing birds we cannot accept. We maintain a core staff to keep our birds healthy and our shelters strong. We also have vet bills, food budgets, and other regular and unexpected expenses to help the Sanctuary and our birds thrive. Settled on one hundred and twenty-two acres near Rhinebeck, New York, Stonehouse Wood Sanctuary is currently home to about five hundred domestic birds.

Many of the birds in our care have been permanently injured and could not survive in the wild. By donating, you enable us to provide the best quality of care we can achieve, together with habitat enhancement and enrichment.

Our mission is to provide refuge and sanctuary to any bird we can accept and nurture. We also support the creatures who live here in the forests and fields around the Sanctuary with a land trust that preserves the natural environment, and allows humans who may come seeking peace to explore our trails. We need your help to keep these lands and streams in their beautiful wild condition and to acquire and protect additional land.

We believe that all life forms deserve respect and are connected in a web that includes all of us. You can join us with a tax-deductible donation, or by sharing this book and our website, scheduling a visit, or simply connecting to nature and birds as you move through the world with wonder.

If you have a bird you think we can help, please contact us. We welcome pigeon, chicken, pheasant, ringneck and diamond dove, or turkeys that need sanctuary; for those domestic creatures, we may be able to help or advise you. (We cannot accept drop-offs; be sure to wait for our reply and then schedule an approved drop-off if we have the available space.)

Please join us in caring for the residents at the Sanctuary with a donation. Any amount you are able to offer will assist us with the daily maintenance and operation of the facility and be warmly welcomed.

If this book has inspired you, donate now at our website, https://stonehousewoodsanctuary.org, or with a check, sent directly to the Sanctuary at: 105 Stonehouse Road, Rhinebeck, NY 12572.

Let us celebrate the magic of birds together!

EXPLORING THE MAGICAL WORLD OF BIRDS

CPSIA information can be obtained
at www.ICGtesting.com
Printed in the USA
JSHW072228070423
40030JS00001B/1